Oh Sweet Day!

A Celebration Cookbook of
Edible Gifts | Party Treats | Festive Desserts

Oh Sweet Day!

A Celebration Cookbook of
Edible Gifts | Party Treats | Festive Desserts

Fanny Lam

Front Table Books | An imprint of Cedar Fort, Inc. | Springville, Utah

ISBN 13: 978-1-4621-2295-0

Published by Front Table Books, an imprint of Cedar Fort, Inc.
2373 W. 700 S., Springville, UT 84663
Distributed by Cedar Fort, Inc., www.cedarfort.com

Library of Congress Cataloging-in-Publication Data

Names: Lam, Fanny, 1974- author.
Title: Oh sweet day! : the celebration cookbook of edible gifts, party
    treats, and festive desserts / Fanny Lam.
Description: Springville, Utah : Front Table Books, An imprint of Cedar Fort,
    Inc., [2018] | Includes index.
Identifiers: LCCN 2018026610 (print) | LCCN 2018027303 (ebook) | ISBN
    9781462129935 (epub, pdf, mobi) | ISBN 9781462122950 (hardback : alk.
    paper)
Subjects: LCSH: Holiday cooking. | LCGFT: Cookbooks.
Classification: LCC TX739 (ebook) | LCC TX739 .L285 2018 (print) | DDC
    641.5/68--dc23
LC record available at https://lccn.loc.gov/2018026610

Cover design by Shawnda T. Craig
Page design by Shawnda T. Craig
Cover design © 2018 Cedar Fort, Inc.
Edited by Sydnee Hyer

Printed in South Korea
10 9 8 7 6 5 4 3 2 1

Printed on acid-free paper

To Matt, Ethan, and Maya

You inspire me not only in the kitchen,
but also in my whole life.

Contents

Happy celebrations, my friends! 1

Cakes

Buns | Breads | Muffins | Breakfast

Pies | Tarts

Cookies | Macarons

Cupcakes | Donuts | Bars

Confections

Happy celebrations, my friends!

Wait! Are you actually celebrating, or are you mostly crumbling under that holiday stress, worrying about what to make for dinner or what to buy for your loved ones?

No matter what you are looking for, my answer for you is "Something sweet." Because calories don't count when it comes to celebrations. That little extra "dessert stomach" will always have room for some delicious sweet treats no matter how much we insist that we are full. And no one will secretly throw away a box of cookies, unlike that useless photo frame still wrapped in its gift box and gathering dust in some forgotten corner of your home.

And if you agree, **this is the book for you!**

Born and raised in a small family in Hong Kong, I have always been reminded that homemade food is the best food. Every day my mother would rush through her busy work schedule as a tailor, go to the market after work to buy the freshest produce and meat, come home, and start cooking while checking our homework at the same time. Before my brother and I finished our reading practice, dinner was ready. A few simple Chinese dishes—nothing fancy, but fresh and tasteful. The three of us would sit and talk over a delightful meal.

The image of my mother juggling work and family as a single parent is definitely one of my vivid childhood memories. As a self-taught tailor, my mother handmade all of our childhood outfits, so unique and stylish, making other parents jealous. Over time, she practiced the necessary handiwork and developed an impeccable sense of aesthetics, which she used to fuel her career, and she became one of the most respected female tailors in her field.

Always energetic, confident, and tenacious, she would knock down any barrier in her way to do her job, and do it better than anyone ever has. She influenced me so deeply!

I carried her dedicated work ethic through my career in a reputable radio station and movie distribution company. I spent most of my twenties organizing concerts, promoting movies, and working with celebrities—such a fulfilling and inspirational job for a fresh college graduate.

Life went on, I grew older, and I started to think about having my own family. I met my husband, Matt, when we were in high school in Hong Kong before he moved to Canada with his family. We maintained a long-distance relationship for a few years. After he finished college, he moved back to Hong Kong for work, and that was when we re-started dating. On and off, we talked about moving back to Canada together. It was around this time that, after a successful career, and despite my love for all the things I grew up with, I decided to leave my hometown, marry Matt, and start my family in Vancouver. That was in 2005.

I spent a lot of time exploring my new city and local culture. Going to the farmer's market was one of the highlights! I would scour the internet for recipes to cook and bake using local ingredients from the market. And that's how I discovered the blogging world. Through this process of self-learning, and being inspired by brilliant bloggers out there, I started to really enjoy my time in the kitchen.

Three years later, my first child, Ethan, was born. Life was hectic for me as a first-time mom. But I could always find comfort in the kitchen. Along the road, I realized that I have a passion for dessert decoration, food styling, and photography, thanks to the immaculate eye of design I inherited from my mother. I jumped on the blogging bandwagon, and created *Oh Sweet Day!*, a blog chronicling my journey as a baker and a mother after I relocated from Hong Kong to Canada. It was an attempt to document stories and memories of food and love for my kids. My grandma chose to spoil us by secretly feeding me Coca-Cola behind my mother's back on my first birthday. My grandma has never been a baking grandma. And I want to be one for my family!

In 2010, our family grew as my daughter, Maya, came along. Cooking has become an important part of our family. Instead of going to restaurants and spending 90% of the time preventing our kids from spilling anything, we enjoyed eating in. We would have friends and family over for backyard barbeque parties, birthdays, and playdates. And there would always be homemade sweets in my house, because gatherings would never be perfect without desserts. Word-of-mouth and rave reviews brought more requests for my baked goods, and also brought on my determination to start a home-based bakery.

It was a family dinner conversation in the fall of 2013 that drove me to create my first *Oh Sweet Day!*'s Holiday Cookie Box, an assortment of handmade gourmet cookies.

From the very first order of a few dozen boxes to over six hundred last Christmas, my signature holiday cookie box has put *Oh Sweet Day!* on the map. Baking over ten thousand cookies, my oven didn't get a chance to cool down. Those two months leading to Christmas were a blur—boxes stacked everywhere in the kitchen, flour and butter all over my shirt, twelve-hour workdays, an aching body, a madness that words cannot describe. But like running a small-but-intimate mom-and-pop shop, I always had my gang—my trusty delivery man and my two little packaging helpers—behind my back. And things did work out beautifully and rewardingly!

I've always loved the idea of giving out edible gifts—something that you can create in your own kitchen instead of bumping around in the crowded shopping mall. It's a very personal way to show that you care, and that you love the person enough to spend a few hours making something unique for them. My client once emailed me, "I might not be able to remember what I received from my Secret Santa last year, but I will always remember your box of cookies! In fact, I was kind of looking forward to receiving it this year!" The best way to a person's heart is through their stomach. And you know, cookies never clutter a space.

One of the many reasons I enjoy baking for my clients is far beyond my passion for baking. It's also about being included in their celebrations. I may be a stranger to them personally, but magically, my desserts are part of their lovely memories. And I will always be grateful for that.

For me, celebrations are a time for sensible creativity that yields comfort, joy, warmth, and good memories of a home-cooked meal, good conversations, silly jokes, music, cheers, and a delightful dessert. My style of baking is friendly and comforting. With a little creativity and heartfelt enthusiasm, I like to make simple desserts look brand new and surprising.

A lovely dessert doesn't require a demanding recipe. It needs love! It needs personality! I hope this book will inspire you to go beyond your comfort zone, try something new, play with abandon, share with your loved one, make it a tradition, and let it be a memory.

let everyday be . . .

Oh
sweet
DAY!

Cakes are a symbol of celebration. Kids blow out candles on them on their birthdays, loving couples slice into them on their wedding day, amazed guests wow over them at dinner parties—cake is magic and happiness! We should celebrate with a cake! Here I serve up classic layered cake, silky mousse cake, decadent cheesecake, easy crowd-pleasing chocolate cake, lovely colorful fruit-filled cake, and petite single-serving cake. Whether you are looking for a party-worthy dessert or simply a rustic treat for any time, I'm sure these all-occasion cakes will inspire smiles and memories.

Cake

Pumpkin Mousse Chocolate Cake

• Makes an 8-inch cake •

Take a break from all the pumpkin pies! This pumpkin dessert is a delightful twist on a traditional holiday dessert that incorporates chocolate, pumpkin, and autumn spices in a pillowy, fluffy, and soft mousse cake. Every bite is like a sweet, flavorful, and luscious puff. It's so light that you might not even need to chew it!

Chocolate Sponge Cake

- ½ cup flour
- 2 Tbsp. cocoa powder
- ¼ tsp. salt
- 3 large eggs, room temperature
- ½ cup granulated sugar
- 1 Tbsp. vegetable oil
- ½ tsp. vanilla extract

Toppings

- ¼ cup chocolate shavings

Pumpkin Mousse

- ¾ Tbsp. unflavored gelatin powder
- ¼ cup cold water
- 2 cups pumpkin purée
- ¼ cup brown sugar
- ½ tsp. ground cinnamon
- ½ tsp. ground ginger
- ¼ tsp. salt
- ½ cup heavy whipping cream
- 3 large egg whites
- 2 Tbsp. granulated sugar

Chocolate Ganache

- 1/3 cup heavy whipping cream
- 100 grams dark chocolate, cut into small pieces

Whipped Cream

- ½ cup heavy whipping cream
- 2 Tbsp. powdered sugar

Chocolate Cake

1. Preheat oven to 325°F. Line the bottom of an 8-inch ungreased cake pan with parchment paper.

2. In a large bowl, sift together the flour, cocoa powder, and salt. Set aside.

3. In the bowl of a standing mixer fitted with a whisk, beat the eggs and sugar on medium speed until light and pale, about 5 minutes.

4. Reduce the speed to low and mix in the flour mixture until just incorporated.

5. Spoon ⅓ cup of the batter in a small bowl. Stir in the oil and vanilla until combined. Pour the mixture back to the mixing bowl. Stir until combined.

6. Pour the batter into the prepared pan. Bake 20 to 25 minutes, until a toothpick inserted in the cake center comes out clean.

7. Let the cake cool in pan for 10 minutes. Remove from pan and let cool completely.

8. Place the cake layer in an 8-inch springform pan.

Pumpkin Mousse Chocolate Cake
(continued)

Pumpkin Mousse

1. Sprinkle the gelatin powder in water. Let stand for 5 minutes. Microwave on high for 20 seconds until the gelatin dissolves. Let cool slightly.

2. In a food processor, mix together the pumpkin purée, brown sugar, cinnamon, ginger, salt, heavy cream, and gelatin mixture until smooth.

3. In the bowl of a standing mixer with a whisk, beat the egg whites on medium speed until foamy. Add sugar and continue beating until firm peaks form.

4. Fold the egg whites in the pumpkin mixture, half at a time, until just incorporated.

5. Pour the pumpkin mixture over the cake into the pan. Jiggle the pan to level the top.

6. Refrigerate the cake overnight.

Chocolate Ganache

1. Microwave the cream on high for 45 seconds. Pour the hot cream over the chocolate. Let sit for a minute, then whisk together until smooth. Let cool slightly.

Whipped Cream

1. Beat the cream and sugar on low speed until soft peaks form. Continue beating on medium speed until firm peaks form.

2. Transfer the whipped cream to a piping bag with a star tip.

Assemble: Release the cake from the pan. Spoon the ganache along the top edges of the cake, and let the ganache drip down to create the drip effect. Pipe the whipped cream over the ganache. Sprinkle the chocolate shavings on top.

Add Some Love...

Make the best pumpkin purée at home with the sweetest Japanese pumpkins. The large field pumpkins are too watery and tasteless. Leave them for jack-o'-lanterns.

Raspberry and Lemon Curd Cream Cake

• Makes an 8-inch two-layer cake •

*A light sponge cake layered with mildly sweetened whipped cream and fresh raspberries.
The creamy and tangy lemon curd gives the cake the extra color and deliciousness.
This all-season dessert guarantees to light up your eyes and tempt your taste buds.*

Lemon Sponge Cake

- 1 cup flour
- ½ tsp. salt
- 6 large eggs,
   room temperature
- 1 cup granulated sugar
- 2 Tbsp. lemon juice
- 1 Tbsp. lemon zest
- 2 Tbsp. vegetable oil
- 1 tsp. vanilla extract

Lemon Curd

- ¼ cup lemon juice
- ½ Tbsp. lemon zest
- ¼ cup granulated sugar
- 1 large egg
- 3 Tbsp. unsalted butter

Whipped Cream

- 1 cup heavy whipping cream
- ¼ cup powdered sugar

Toppings

- ½ cup fresh raspberries

Lemon Sponge Cake

1. Preheat oven to 325°F. Line the bottom of an 8-inch ungreased cake pan with parchment paper.

2. In a large bowl, sift together the flour and salt. Set aside.

3. In the bowl of a standing mixer fitted with a whisk, beat the eggs and sugar on medium speed until light and pale, about 5 minutes.

4. Mix in the lemon juice and zest until combined.

5. Reduce the mixer speed to low and mix in the flour mixture until just incorporated.

6. Spoon ½ cup batter into a small bowl; stir in the oil and vanilla until combined. Pour the mixture back to the mixing bowl. Stir until combined.

7. Pour the batter into the prepared pan. Bake 25 to 30 minutes, until a toothpick inserted in the cake center comes out clean.

8. Let the cake cool in pan for 10 minutes. Remove from pan and let cool completely.

9. Slice the cake horizontally into 2 layers.

Add Some Love...

You can go with almost any berries you prefer. Mixed berries will definitely boost up the stunning level of this lovely dessert.

Lemon Curd

1. Cook the lemon juice, zest, sugar, and egg on low heat while whisking for 10 minutes, until thickened.

2. Remove from heat. Mix in the butter until combined.

3. Strain the lemon curd to make it smooth.

4. Let cool to room temperature.

Whipped Cream

1. In a medium bowl, beat together the cream and sugar on low speed until soft peaks form. Continue beating on medium speed until firm peaks form.

Assemble: Place one cake layer on the serving plate. Spread half of the whipped cream on top. Drizzle the lemon curd over the whipped cream. Scatter half of the raspberries on top. Repeat with another cake layer, whipped cream, lemon curd, and raspberries.

Salted Caramel Cheesecake Bars

• Makes 20 squares •

Buttery and nutty shortbread crust. Creamy and velvety cream cheese layer.
Sweet and salty caramel sauce. Petite and elegant presentation. I mean, do I need to say more?

Pecan Shortbread Crust

2/3 cup pecans, toasted and
   roughly chopped
6 Tbsp. unsalted butter, cold
   and cut into small pieces
¾ cup and 2 Tbsp. flour
1/3 cup granulated sugar
1 tsp. salt

Cheesecake

1 cup cream cheese,
   softened
1 cup sour cream, room
   temperature
½ cup granulated sugar
2 large eggs, room
   temperature
1 tsp. vanilla extract
½ tsp. salt

Salted Caramel

½ cup granulated sugar
2 Tbsp. water
3 Tbsp. unsalted butter
¼ cup heavy whipping
   cream
2 tsp. sea salt flakes

Pecan Shortbread Crust

1. Preheat oven to 350°F. Grease and line an 8-inch square baking pan with parchment paper.

2. In a food processor, mix together all the ingredients until the mixture resembles wet sand. Press the mixture onto the bottom of the prepared pan.

3. Bake the crust for 15 to 20 minutes. Let cool completely.

Cheesecake

1. Lower the oven temperature to 250°F.

2. In a clean food processor, blend together the cream cheese, sour cream, and sugar until combined.

3. Mix in the eggs, one at a time, followed by the vanilla and salt.

4. Pour the filling over the cooled crust into the pan. Tap the pan on the counter a few times to remove the air bubbles in the batter. Bake the cheesecake for 40 to 45 minutes, until the edge of the cheesecake is puffed but the center is still wobbly and wet-looking.

5. Turn off the oven with the door slightly open. Let the cheesecake sit in the oven to cool completely, at least an hour.

6. Refrigerate the cheesecake overnight.

Salted Caramel

1. Cook the sugar and water on low heat until the sugar is dissolved.

2. Add the butter. Let it come to a boil and cook until the mixture reaches a golden caramel color.

3. Remove from heat and whisk in the cream slowly. Mix in a teaspoon of sea salt.

4. Let cool to room temperature.

Assemble: Pour the caramel over the cooled cheesecake. Refrigerate the cake for 30 minutes.

Release the cheesecake from the pan. Cut into squares. Sprinkle the remaining sea salt on top.

Add Some Love...

Try to make friends with sea salt flakes. These snow-white, ocean-scented, pyramid-shaped crystals will make your desserts, especially chocolate desserts, look a million times more elegant!

Chocolate Ganache Cake

• Makes an 8-inch 3-layer cake •

A big shout out to all chocolate lovers! Also to all the hosts who have no idea what dessert you should make for the party! Because who doesn't love chocolate? Decadent chocolate cake layers with rich and creamy chocolate ganache frosting make this cake a true indulgence. Chocolate ganache is simply made of chocolate and heavy whipping cream. Its versatility as a glaze, decorative piping, and frosting answers all the needs for cake decoration.

Devil's Food Cake

3 cups cake flour
2 tsp. baking powder
1 tsp. baking soda
½ tsp. salt
½ cup boiling water
¾ cup cocoa powder
1½ cups unsalted butter, softened
2 cups light brown sugar

4 large eggs, room temperature
1 cup buttermilk, room temperature
1 Tbsp. vanilla extract

Chocolate Ganache Frosting

1 1/3cups heavy whipping cream
400 grams dark chocolate, cut into
  small pieces

Devil's Food Cake

1. Preheat oven to 350°F. Grease and line the bottoms of three 8-inch cake pans with parchment paper.

2. In a large bowl, whisk together the flour, baking powder, baking soda, and salt. Set aside.

3. In a small bowl, whisk together the boiling water and cocoa powder until smooth.

4. In the bowl of a standing mixer fitted with a paddle attachment, beat the butter and sugar on medium speed until light and fluffy, about 5 minutes.

5. Beat in the eggs, one at a time, followed by the buttermilk and vanilla.

6. Reduce the speed to low and mix in half of the flour mixture, the cocoa mixture, and the remaining half of the flour mixture. Mix until just incorporated between each addition.

7. Evenly divide the batter among the prepared pans. Bake 15 to 20 minutes, until a toothpick inserted in the cake center comes out clean.

8. Let the cakes cool in pans for 10 minutes. Remove from pans and let cool completely.

Chocolate Ganache Frosting

1. Microwave the cream on high for 45 seconds.

2. Pour the hot cream over the chocolate. Let sit for a minute, and then whisk together until smooth.

3. Let cool until it reaches a thick but spreadable consistency.

4. Reserve ¼ cup of frosting for decoration.

Assemble: Place one cake layer on the serving plate. Spread the frosting on top. Place another cake layer over the frosting. Gently press down a little. Repeat with the frosting. Place the final cake layer on top. Frost the top and sides with the remaining ganache. Warm the reserved ganache in microwave for 10 seconds. Spoon the ganache along the top edges of the cake, and let it drip down to create the drip effect.

Add Some Love...

Decorate the cake with anything chocolatey— leftover Halloween chocolates, sprinkles, cookies, chocolate-coated nuts, chocolate truffles, or something as simple as chunks of chocolate bars.

Coconut Crepe Cake with Banana Cream

• Makes a 7-inch 20-layer cake •

Both festive and cozy at once, crepe cake is always a delightful and sophisticated dessert that will impress even the most experienced bakers at the table. In this version, I layer the crepes with a rich filling of banana pastry cream and frost the whole cake with coconut whipped cream. I guarantee you won't be able to have just one slice.

Banana Pastry Cream

2 cups milk
1 tsp. vanilla extract
3 egg yolks
1/3 cup granulated sugar
¼ cup cornstarch
2 ripe bananas, mashed

Crepes

6 Tbsp. unsalted butter, melted and cooled
2 1/3 cups milk

6 large eggs
1½ cups flour
½ tsp. salt
½ cup granulated sugar

Coconut Whipped Cream

2 cups heavy whipping cream
¼ cup powdered sugar
1 cup unsweetened coconuts, lightly toasted

Banana Pastry Cream

1. In a saucepan, cook the milk and vanilla on medium heat to bring the mixture just to a boil. Stir occasionally.

2. In a small bowl, whisk together the egg yolks and sugar until the mixture becomes light and fluffy.

3. Whisk in the cornstarch until smooth.

4. Slowly whisk in one third of the milk mixture to the egg mixture. Pour the milk-egg mixture back to the saucepan. Cook on low heat and whisk continuously until the custard is thickened, about 3 minutes.

5. Strain the custard to make it smooth.

6. Mix in the mashed bananas until combined.

7. Let cool to room temperature.

8. Place a plastic wrap directly on the surface of the banana pastry cream.

9. Refrigerate until ready to use.

Coconut Crepe Cake with Banana Cream
(continued)

Crepes

1. In a food processor, mix together all the ingredients until smooth.

2. Cover the batter with plastic wrap. Refrigerate for an hour.

3. Heat a 7-inch skillet over medium heat with a light coating of oil.

4. Pour ¼ cup of batter into the skillet, swirling it until it evenly coats the bottom. Let it cook undisturbed until the bottom is golden and the top is set, about a minute. Carefully flip to another side and cook for 15 to 20 seconds.

5. Transfer the crepe to a cookie pan to cool.

6. Continue with the remaining batter. Stack the crepes and let cool completely.

Coconut Whipped Cream

1. In the bowl of a standing mixer fitted with a whisk, beat the cream and sugar on low speed until soft peaks form. Continue beating on medium speed until firm peaks form. Refrigerate the whipped cream until ready to use.

Assemble: Place a crepe on the serving plate. Spread 2 to 3 tablespoons of pastry cream on top. Repeat with all the crepes until the last one is placed.

Frost the top and sides of the cake with the coconut whipped cream. Cover the cake with toasted coconuts.

Chill the cake in the refrigerator before serving.

Add Some Love...

You might want to showcase the beautiful crepe layers instead of covering the whole cake with whipped cream. Why not? Just skip the frosting part, and place a big cloud of whipped cream on top of the crepe cake with a sprinkle of toasted coconuts.

Chocolate Lava Cakes

• Makes six 3-inch cakes •

My son doesn't like chocolate. But as strange as it sounds, he does love my chocolate lava cake. I guess this warm, gooey, and luscious dessert is not only a chocolate lover's dream; its super chocolate power can also win some chocolate haters' hearts.

Chocolate Lava Cakes

120 grams dark chocolate, cut into pieces
2/3 cup unsalted butter
4 large eggs
2/3 cup granulated sugar

1 tsp. vanilla extract
½ cup flour
1 Tbsp. powdered sugar

Chocolate Lava Cakes

1. Grease six 3-inch ramekins. Line the bottoms with parchment paper.

2. Set a bowl over a pan of simmering water. Stir and melt together the chocolate and butter until smooth.

3. Let cool for 10 minutes.

4. In the bowl of a standing mixer fitted with a whisk, beat the eggs and sugar on medium speed until thick and pale.

5. Mix in the vanilla until combined.

6. Mix in the flour until just incorporated.

7. Mix in the chocolate mixture slowly until combined.

8. Evenly divide the batter among the prepared ramekins. Refrigerate until ready to serve.

9. Preheat oven to 400°F. Bake the cakes for 15 minutes, or until the top is set.

10. Let cool for 5 minutes. Invert the cakes onto the individual serving plates. Remove the parchment paper.

11. Sprinkle the powdered sugar on top.

Add Some Love...

You can prepare the cakes the day before. Chill the batter in the refrigerator and bake when ready to serve. This means you will have time to prepare the toppings! Make some whipped cream, salted caramel (recipe on page 16), or simply go down to the grocery and buy some fresh berries and vanilla ice cream.

Fall Spice Cake with Lemon Cream Cheese Frosting

• Makes an 8-inch 2-layer cake •

It would not be a holiday season at our house without the smell of cinnamon in the kitchen. This cake, packed with the fall spice aroma, is incredibly moist and flavorful. The slight tang of the cream cheese with a vibrant lemon punch provides a complementary note to this heart-warming dessert on any chilling autumn day.

Fall Spice Cake

2 cups flour
2 tsp. baking powder
1 tsp. baking soda
½ tsp. salt
1 tsp. ground cinnamon
1 tsp. ground ginger
1 tsp. freshly grated nutmeg
½ cup granulated sugar
½ cup vegetable oil
½ cup honey
1 large egg, room temperature
1 tsp. vanilla extract
1 cup sour cream, room temperature

Lemon Cream Cheese Frosting

1 cup cream cheese, softened
½ cup unsalted butter, softened
1 Tbsp. lemon juice
1 cup powdered sugar

Fall Spice Cake

1. Preheat oven to 350°F. Grease and line the bottoms of two 8-inch cake pans with parchment paper.

2. In a large bowl, whisk together the flour, baking powder, baking soda, salt, and spices.

3. In the bowl of a standing mixer fitted with a paddle attachment, beat the sugar, oil, and honey on medium speed until light and fluffy, about 5 minutes.

4. Beat in the egg, followed by the vanilla.

5. Reduce the speed to low and gradually mix in half of the flour mixture, all of the sour cream, and the remaining half of the flour mixture. Mix until just incorporated between each addition.

6. Evenly divide the batter among the prepared pans. Bake 15 to 20 minutes, until a toothpick inserted in the cake center comes out clean.

7. Let the cakes cool in pans for 10 minutes. Remove from pans and let cool completely.

Lemon Cream Cheese Frosting

1. In the bowl of a standing mixer fitted with a paddle attachment, beat the cream cheese, butter, and lemon juice on medium speed for a few minutes.

2. Add the powdered sugar and continue beating on low speed until the sugar is incorporated. Turn up the speed to medium and beat the frosting until light and fluffy, about 5 minutes.

Assemble: Place one cake layer on the serving plate. Spread the frosting on top. Place another cake layer over the frosting. Gently press down a little. Frost the top and sides with the remaining frosting.

Add Some Love...

Add a lovely and elegant touch to this simple cake by adding some lemon slices, cinnamon sticks, rosemary springs, toasted pecans, etc.

Mini Peanut Butter Cheesecakes with Toasted Marshmallow Frosting

• Makes six 3-inch cakes •

If you think peanut butter and cheesecake already make a perfect marriage, imagine adding toasted marshmallow frosting. Nothing can beat this lovely union of sweetness, saltiness, and fluffiness.

Graham Cracker Crust

1¼ cups graham cracker crumbs
¼ cup unsalted butter, melted

Peanut Butter Cheesecake Filling

1 cup cream cheese, softened
¼ cup smooth peanut butter

¼ cup brown sugar
1 large egg, room temperature
½ tsp. vanilla extract

Toasted Marshmallow Frosting

½ cup granulated sugar
2 egg whites
½ tsp. vanilla extract

Graham Cracker Crust

1. Preheat oven to 350°F. Grease mini cheesecake pans with removable bottoms.

2. Mix together all the ingredients until the mixture resembles wet sand. Press the mixture evenly onto the bottoms of the prepared cheesecake pans.

3. Bake the crust for 10 to 15 minutes. Let cool completely.

Peanut Butter Cheesecake Filling

1. Lower the oven temperature to 250°F.

2. In a food processor, blend together the cream cheese, peanut butter, and brown sugar until combined.

3. Mix in the egg and vanilla until combined.

4. Pour the filling evenly over the cooled crusts in the pans.

5. Bake the cheesecakes for 20 to 25 minutes, until the tops of the cheesecakes are lightly puffed.

6. Turn off the oven with the door slightly opened. Let the cheesecakes sit in the oven to cool completely, for at least an hour.

7. Refrigerate the cheesecakes overnight.

Toasted Marshmallow Frosting

1. Set the bowl of a standing mixer over a pan of simmering water. Whisk the sugar and egg whites until the sugar is dissolved and the egg whites are warm to touch.

2. Transfer the bowl to the standing mixer fitted with a whisk, beat on high speed until the frosting forms firm peaks.

3. Mix in vanilla until combined.

4. Transfer the frosting to a piping bag with a round tip.

5. Assemble: Release the cheesecakes from the pan. Pipe the frosting on top of each cake. Use a kitchen torch to lightly brown the frosting.

Add Some Love...

No worries if you don't have a kitchen torch. The marshmallow frosting tastes as lovely untoasted. Instead, try scattering some chopped peanuts on the frosting for the crunch.

Orange Almond Cake with Crème Fraîche

• Makes an 8-inch cake •

This buttery almond cake is remarkably light and tender. Instead of using almond flour, try grinding whole and skin-on almonds to give the cake its rustic and nutty texture. The orange flavor really shines through, thanks to the addition of fresh orange juice and zest. This cake requires no icing, but you will love that extra dollop of mildly sweetened crème fraîche.

Almond Cake

1 cup flour

½ cup ground almonds

2 tsp. baking powder

½ tsp. salt

¼ cup unsalted butter, softened

½ cup granulated sugar

2 large eggs, room temperature

1 tsp. vanilla extract

½ cup orange juice

1 Tbsp. orange zest

Orange Crème Fraîche Topping

1 cup crème fraîche

1 Tbsp. powdered sugar

1 Tbsp. orange zest

Toppings

¼ cup sliced almonds

Orange Almond Cake

1. Preheat oven to 350°F. Grease and line the bottom of an 8-inch cake pan with parchment paper.

2. In a large bowl, whisk together the flour, almonds, baking powder, and salt.

3. In the bowl of a standing mixer fitted with a paddle attachment, beat the butter and sugar on medium speed until light and fluffy, about 5 minutes.

4. Beat in the eggs, one at a time, followed by the vanilla.

5. Reduce the speed to low and mix in half of the flour mixture, the orange juice and zest, and the remaining half of the flour mixture. Mix until just incorporated between each addition.

6. Pour the batter into the prepared pan. Bake 20 to 25 minutes, until a toothpick inserted in the cake center comes out clean.

7. Let the cake cool in pan for 10 minutes. Remove from pan and let cool completely.

Orange Crème Fraîche

1. Mix together the crème fraîche, powdered sugar, and orange zest until smooth.

2. Top the cake with the orange crème fraîche. Sprinkle the sliced almonds on top.

Add Some Love...

If crème fraîche sounds a little foreign to you, try whipped cream or cream cheese frosting.

Chocolate Raspberry Dream Cake

• Makes a 6-inch 3-layer cake •

Chocolate and berries are such good friends! The sweetness and fruitiness from the little berries balances the richness of dark chocolate beautifully. Not only does this combination make for a flavorful dessert, but the vibrant colors also make a gorgeous-looking treat. This beauty has a pillowy and naturally pink whipped cream hidden between layers of decadent chocolate cake and inside a blanket of chocolate buttercream, making a lovely and dreamy presentation when sliced.

Devil's Food Cake

1½ cups cake flour
1 tsp. baking powder
½ tsp. baking soda
½ tsp. salt
¼ cup hot water
¼ cup cocoa powder
¾ cup unsalted butter, softened
1 cup light brown sugar
2 large eggs, room temperature
½ cup buttermilk, room temperature
½ Tbsp. vanilla extract

Raspberry Whipped Cream Filling

½ cup heavy whipping cream
2 Tbsp. powdered sugar
1 Tbsp. raspberry purée
½ cup fresh raspberries

Chocolate Buttercream

1 cup unsalted butter, softened
2 cups powdered sugar, sifted
½ cup cocoa powder, sifted

Chocolate Ganache

1/3 cup heavy whipping cream
100 grams dark chocolate, cut into small pieces

Toppings

½ cup fresh raspberries

Chocolate Raspberry Dream Cake
(continued)

Devil's Food Cake

1. Preheat oven to 350°F. Grease and line the bottoms of three 6-inch cake pans with parchment paper.

2. In a large bowl, whisk together the flour, baking powder, baking soda, and salt.

3. In a small bowl, whisk together the hot water and cocoa powder until smooth.

4. In the bowl of a standing mixer fitted with a paddle attachment, beat the butter and sugar on medium speed until light and fluffy, about 5 minutes.

5. Beat the eggs into the butter-sugar mixture, one at a time, followed by the buttermilk and vanilla.

6. Reduce the speed to low and mix in half of the flour mixture, the cocoa mixture, and the remaining half of the flour mixture. Mix until just incorporated between each addition.

7. Evenly divide the batter among the prepared pans. Bake 10 to 15 minutes, until a toothpick inserted in the cake center comes out clean.

8. Let the cakes cool in pans for 10 minutes. Remove from pans and let cool completely.

Raspberry Whipped Cream Filling

1. In the bowl of a standing mixer fitted with a whisk, beat the cream and sugar on low speed until soft peaks form. Add the raspberry purée and continue beating on medium speed until firm peaks form. Refrigerate the whipped cream until ready to use.

Chocolate Buttercream

1. In the bowl of a standing mixer fitted with a paddle attachment, beat the butter on medium speed for 2 minutes.

2. Add the sugar and cocoa powder and continue beating on low speed until the dry ingredients are incorporated. Turn up the speed to medium, and beat the buttercream until light and fluffy, about 5 minutes.

3. Transfer the buttercream to a piping bag with a round tip.

Chocolate Ganache

1. Microwave the cream on high for 45 seconds.

2. Pour the hot cream over the chocolate. Let sit for a minute, and then whisk together until smooth.

3. Let cool slightly.

Assemble: Place one cake layer on the serving plate. Pipe the buttercream along the top edges of the cake. Fill in with half of the raspberry cream filling and half of the fresh raspberries. Place another cake layer on top. Gently press down a little. Repeat with the buttercream, the remaining raspberry cream, and the raspberries. Place the last cake layer on top. Frost the top and sides with the remaining buttercream. Pour the ganache over the cake. Use a spatula to quickly push the ganache over the edges of the cake, and let the ganache drip down to create the drip effect. Top with fresh raspberries.

Add Some Love...

I like to decorate my chocolate cakes with edible gold leaf. Not as expensive as it looks, this pure, natural gold can easily be found online.

Mini Chocolate Peanut Butter Cakes

• Makes six 3-inch cakes •

*Chocolate and peanut butter are such powerful partners in crime that they can hijack willpower.
When it comes to cake, the rich, tantalizing taste of chocolate and the sweet,
nutty taste of peanut butter are essentially a flavor power couple.*

Chocolate Cake

1 cup flour
¼ cup cocoa powder, sifted
1 cup granulated sugar
1 tsp. baking powder
1 tsp. baking soda
½ tsp. salt
1 large egg, room temperature
½ cup sour cream, room temperature
¼ cup vegetable oil
1 Tbsp. vanilla extract
½ cup hot water

Peanut Butter Buttercream

1½ cups smooth peanut butter
½ cup unsalted butter, softened
2 cups powdered sugar
1 tsp. vanilla extract
¼ cup heavy whipping cream

Chocolate Ganache

1/3 cup heavy whipping cream
100 grams dark chocolate, cut into small
  pieces

Toppings

2 Tbsp. salted peanuts, roughly chopped

Chocolate Cake

1. Preheat oven to 350°F. Grease and line a 9x13 baking pan with parchment paper.

2. Whisk together the flour, cocoa powder, sugar, baking powder, baking soda, and salt.

3. Stir in the egg, sour cream, oil, and vanilla until combined.

4. Mix in the hot water slowly until the mixture becomes smooth.

5. Pour the batter into the prepared pan. Bake for 15 to 20 minutes, until a toothpick inserted in the cake center comes out clean.

6. Let the cake cool in pan for 10 minutes. Invert the cake and let cool completely.

7. Use a 3-inch cookie cutter to cut out 12 cake circles.

8. Freeze the cake circles for 10 minutes for easy frosting.

Mini Chocolate Peanut Butter Cakes
(continued)

Peanut Butter Buttercream

1. In the bowl of a standing mixer with a paddle attachment, beat the peanut butter and butter on medium speed for 2 minutes.

2. Add the sugar; continue beating on low speed until the sugar is incorporated.

3. Add the vanilla and cream and beat on medium speed until the buttercream is light and fluffy, about 5 minutes.

Chocolate Ganache

1. Microwave the cream on high for 45 seconds.

2. Pour the hot cream over the chocolate. Let sit for a minute, and then whisk together until smooth.

3. Let cool slightly.

Assemble: Sandwich two cake circles with 2–3 tablespoons buttercream. Frost the top and sides of each cake with the remaining buttercream. Pour the ganache over the cake. Use a spatula to quickly push the ganache over the edges of the cake, and let the ganache drip down to cover the whole cake. Repeat with all the cakes. Sprinkles the peanuts on top.

Add Some Love...

Instead of only two layers, stack three or even four layers together to make a taller and more chic-looking cake if you prefer.

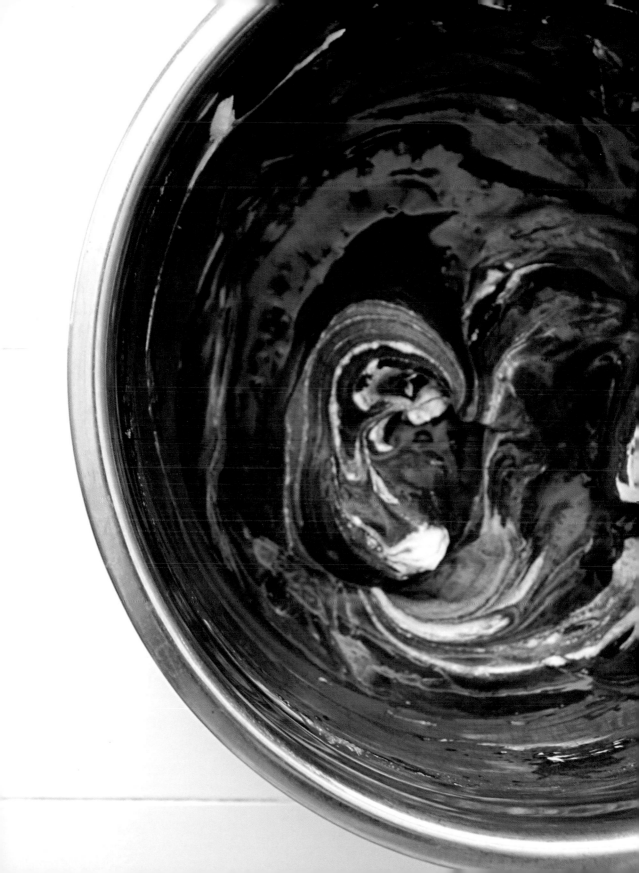

Mixed Berries and Chocolate Cream Cake

• Makes a 3-layer cake •

Fresh berries are your best helpers when it comes to easily creating a beautiful and delicious cake
The colorful berries go perfectly with silky vanilla whipped cream and decadent chocolate cake layers.
Get the extra boost from the gorgeous drips of chocolate ganache.

Devil's Food Cake

1½ cups cake flour
1 tsp. baking powder
½ tsp. baking soda
½ tsp. salt
¼ cup hot water
¼ cup cocoa powder
¾ cup unsalted butter, softened
1 cup light brown sugar
2 large eggs, room temperature
½ cup buttermilk, room temperature
½ Tbsp. vanilla extract

Mixed Berries Whipped Cream Filling

2 cups heavy whipping cream
¼ cup powdered sugar
1 cup fresh berries

Chocolate Ganache

1/3 cup heavy whipping cream
100 grams dark chocolate, cut into small pieces

Toppings

1 cup fresh berries
1 Tbsp. powdered sugar

Devil's Food Cake

1. Preheat oven to 350°F. Grease and line a 9x13 cookie sheet pan with parchment paper.

2. In a large bowl, whisk together the flour, baking powder, baking soda, and salt.

3. In another bowl, whisk together the hot water and cocoa powder until smooth.

4. In the bowl of a standing mixer fitted with a paddle attachment, beat the butter and sugar on medium speed until light and fluffy, about 5 minutes.

5. Beat in the eggs, one at a time, followed by the buttermilk and vanilla.

6. Reduce the speed to low and mix in half of the flour mixture, the cocoa mixture, and the remaining half of the flour mixture. Mix until just incorporated between each addition.

7. Pour the batter into the prepared pan. Bake 15 to 20 minutes, until a toothpick inserted in the cake center comes out clean.

8. Let the cakes cool in pan for 10 minutes. Invert the cake, and let cool completely.

9. Cut the cake into three 9x4-inch rectangles.

Mixed Berries and Chocolate Cream Cake
(continued)

Mixed Berries Whipped Cream Filling

1. In the bowl of a standing mixer fitted with a whisk, beat the cream and sugar on low speed until soft peaks form. Continue beating on medium speed until firm peaks form. Refrigerate the whipped cream until ready to use.

Chocolate Ganache

1. Microwave the cream on high for 45 seconds. Pour the hot cream over the chocolate. Let sit for a minute, and then whisk together until combined and smooth. Let cool slightly.

Assemble: Place one cake layer on the serving plate. Spread the whipped cream on top. Scatter the berries over the cream. Place another cake layer on top. Gently press down a little. Repeat with the whipped cream and berries. Place the last cake layer on top. Frost the top and sides with the remaining whipped cream. Pour the ganache over the cake. Use a spatula to quickly push the ganache over the edges of the cake, and let the ganache drip down to create the drip effect. Top with the berries. Sprinkle the powdered sugar over the berries.

Add Some Love...

Double the stunning effect by decorating the cake with chocolate-covered strawberries!

Orange Hazelnut Cheesecake

• Makes a 9-inch cake •

My winning formula for a perfect cheesecake is to bake it at a very low temperature for a longer period of time. My cheesecake is silky, smooth, and crack-free every single time. No annoying waterbath required! Once you are able to tackle this challenge, it's only natural to inject creativity in your cheesecakes, like this orange hazelnut variation.

Orange Hazelnut Shortbread Crust

½ cup unsalted butter

¼ cup powdered sugar

2 Tbsp. orange zest

¼ cup hazelnuts, finely chopped

1 cup all-purpose flour

¼ tsp. salt

Cheesecake

2 cups cream cheese, softened

1 cup sour cream, room temperature

2 Tbsp. orange juice

1 cup granulated sugar

3 large eggs, separated, room temperature

1 Tbsp. vanilla extract

½ tsp. salt

Whipped Cream

½ cup heavy whipping cream

2 Tbsp. powdered sugar

Toppings

10 orange slices

¼ cup hazelnuts, roughly chopped

Orange Hazelnut Shortbread Crust

1. Preheat oven to 350°F. Line the bottom of a 9-inch ungreased springform pan with parchment paper.

2. In the bowl of a standing mixer fitted with a paddle attachment, beat the butter and sugar on medium speed until light and fluffy, about 5 minutes.

3. Mix in the orange zest until combined.

4. Add the hazelnuts. Sift in the flour and salt. Mix on low speed until just incorporated.

5. Press the mixture onto the bottom of the prepared pan. Bake the crust for 15 to 20 minutes. Let cool completely.

Orange Hazelnut Cheesecake
(continued)

Cheesecake

1. Lower the oven temperature to 250°F.

2. In a food processor, blend together the cream cheese, sour cream, orange juice, and sugar until combined.

3. Mix in the egg yolks, one at a time, followed by the vanilla and salt.

4. In a big bowl, whisk the egg whites until soft peaks form.

5. Fold the egg whites in the cheesecake mixture, half at a time, until just incorporated. Pour the filling over the cooled crust into the pan. Tap the pan on the counter a few times to remove the air bubbles in the batter.

6. Bake the cheesecake for 80 to 90 minutes, until the edge of the cheesecake is puffed but the center is still wobbly and wet looking.

7. Turn off the oven with the door slightly opened. Let the cheesecake sit in the oven to cool completely, at least an hour.

8. Refrigerate the cheesecake overnight.

Whipped Cream

1. In the bowl of a standing mixer fitted with a whisk, beat the cream and sugar on low speed until soft peaks form. Continue beating on medium speed until firm peaks form.

Assemble: Release the cake from the pan. Spread the whipped cream over the cake. Garnish with the orange slices and hazelnuts.

Add Some Love...

Whipped cream gives cheesecake a delightful and airy touch. No one will say no to this lovely addition to an already wonderful dessert.

Triple Chocolate Mousse Cake

• Makes an 8-inch cake •

Fluffy and airy chocolate sponge cake + smooth and creamy
dark chocolate mousse + decadent chocolate ganache = Triple Chocolate Heaven!

Chocolate Sponge Cake

½ cup flour

2 Tbsp. cocoa powder

¼ tsp. salt

3 large eggs, room temperature

½ cup granulated sugar

1 Tbsp. vegetable oil

½ tsp. vanilla extract

Chocolate Mousse

200 grams dark chocolate, cut into small
   pieces

1 Tbsp. unsalted butter

¼ cup water

3 eggs, separated

1 Tbsp. granulated sugar

1 cup heavy whipping cream

Chocolate Ganache

100 grams dark chocolate, cut into small
   pieces

1/3 cup heavy whipping cream

Toppings

¼ cup chocolate curls

Chocolate Sponge Cake

1. Preheat the oven to 325°F. Line the bottom of an 8-inch ungreased cake pan with parchment paper.

2. In a large bowl, sift together the flour, cocoa powder, and salt.

3. In a bowl of a standing mixer fitted with a whisk, beat the eggs and sugar on medium speed until light and pale, about 5 minutes.

4. Reduce the speed to low and mix in the flour mixture until just incorporated.

5. Spoon 1/3 cup of the batter in a small bowl and stir in the oil and vanilla until combined. Pour the mixture back to the mixing bowl. Stir until combined.

6. Pour the batter into the prepared pan. Bake 20 to 25 minutes, until a toothpick inserted in the cake center comes out clean.

7. Let the cake cool in the pan for 10 minutes. Remove from pan and let cool completely.

Triple Chocolate Mousse Cake
(continued)

Chocolate Mousse

1. Combine the chocolate, butter, and water in a heatproof bowl set over a pan of simmering water. Whisk constantly until the mixture is smooth. Let cool slightly.

2. In the bowl of a standing mixer fitted with a whisk, beat the egg whites on medium speed until foamy. Add the sugar and continue beating until firm peaks form. Transfer to another bowl.

3. In the same bowl of a standing mixer, beat the egg yolks until light and fluffy. Slowly mix in the chocolate mixture. Fold the whipped egg whites in the chocolate mixture. In another large bowl, whip the cream until firm peaks form. Fold the whipped cream in the chocolate mixture until combined.

Chocolate Ganache

1. Microwave the cream on high for 45 seconds.

2. Pour the hot cream over the chocolate. Let sit for a minute, and then whisk together until smooth. Let cool slightly.

3. Pour the ganache over the chilled mousse cake. Let it set for 10 minutes.

4. Remove the cake from the pan.

5. Sprinkle the chocolate curls around the top edges of the cake.

Assemble: Place the cake layer in an 8-inch springform pan. Pour the chocolate mixture over the cake. Jiggle to level the top. Refrigerate the cake overnight.

Add Some Love...

Like I always say, chocolate and berries are very good friends. Top your already amazing cake with some bright red strawberries!

For me, holidays are not for sleeping in, but for long, leisurely breakfasts that fill my house with the aromas of freshly baked breads, sweet buns, warm eggs, and sizzling bacon. Holiday breakfasts are all about celebrating the season with cozy autumn spices and produce: soft and buttery cinnamon brioche, pumpkin muffins with cream cheese filling and walnut streusel, and apple fritter monkey bread. Or bring some chic and beauty to your breakfast table with double chocolate raspberry muffins, lemon blueberry Dutch baby pancakes, and raspberry almond scones. These recipes will make breakfast or brunch the meal you dream about at night and cannot wait to wake up for.

Buns | Breads
Muffins | Breakfast

Cinnamon Brioche Wreath

• Makes a 10-inch wreath •

Soft and buttery, brioche is a lovely cross between bread and pastry, thanks to the high content of butter and eggs. The dough requires overnight rising to slow the fermentation. Also, the chilled butter makes the dough easier to shape. With a little more love, you can easily transform humble ingredients into a beautiful and delicious braided bread to enjoy with your loved ones!

Dough

½ cup milk, warm (110°F)

3 Tbsp. granulated sugar

2¼ tsp. active dry yeast

4 large eggs, room temperature

3½ cups flour

2 tsp. salt

¾ cup unsalted butter, softened and cut
   into small pieces

Filling

¼ cup unsalted butter, melted

½ cup granulated sugar

3 tsp. ground cinnamon

Egg Wash

1 egg yolk

1 Tbsp. heavy whipping cream

Dough

1. In the bowl of a standing mixer fitted with a paddle attachment, mix together the milk and sugar. Sprinkle the yeast over the mixture. Let sit for 10 minutes.

2. Mix in the eggs, one at a time, until the mixture becomes light and creamy.

3. Mix in the flour and salt until just incorporated.

4. Slowly mix in the butter pieces. Let the mixer knead the dough until it becomes very stretchy and sticky, about 5 minutes.

5. Place the dough in a lightly oiled large bowl. Cover and let rise for 2 hours.

6. Refrigerate the dough overnight. Remove the dough from the refrigerator the next day. Let it come to room temperature.

7. On a well-floured surface, flatten and roll the dough into a 20x28-inch rectangle.

Cinnamon Brioche Wreath
(continued)

Filling

1. Brush the dough evenly with the melted butter.

2. Mix together the sugar and cinnamon. Sprinkle the mixture over the butter.

3. Beginning with the long side, roll the dough into a log. Pinch the seam together at the end.

4. Cut the log in half lengthwise. With the cut sides facing up, gently press together one end of each half. Start placing one half over another until the entire roll is twisted. Press the ends together to seal. Shape the twisted dough into a circle. Fold the ends under each other to resemble a braid.

5. Place the dough on a baking pan lined with the parchment paper. Cover and let rise for another hour.

Egg Wash

1. Mix together the yolk and cream. Lightly brush the egg wash over the dough.

2. Preheat oven to 350°F. Bake the brioche wreath for 30 to 35 minutes, until golden brown.

3. Let cool slightly before slicing.

Add Some Love...

Make your brioche more flavorful and beautiful by adding some dried fruits, chocolate chips, or nuts in the filling. Or simply drizzle some icing on top.

"Love Someone" Banana Bread

• Makes one loaf •

We all love banana bread! You may not be a cake maker, but you can definitely whip up a good loaf of banana bread with some special add-ins exclusive for your loved ones and declare, "Here, I baked you something from scratch because I love you!"

1¾ cups flour
1 tsp. baking powder
1 tsp. baking soda
½ tsp. salt
3 large eggs, room temperature
¾ cup granulated sugar

2 large overripe bananas, mashed
¾ cup vegetable oil
¾ cup desired add-in (chocolate chips, coconut flakes, nuts, seeds, rolled oats, or dried fruits)

"Love Someone" Banana Bread

1. Preheat oven to 350°F. Grease and line a loaf pan with parchment paper.

2. In a large bowl, whisk together the flour, baking powder, baking soda and salt.

3. In another large bowl, whisk together the eggs, sugar, bananas, and oil until combined.

4. Stir in the flour mixture until just incorporated.

5. Fold in your loved one's favorite add-in.

6. Pour the batter into the prepared pan. Bake 55 to 60 minutes, until a toothpick inserted in the center comes out clean.

7. Let cool in pan for 10 minutes. Remove from pan, and let cool completely.

Add Some Love...

This is my mother-in-law's favorite banana bread. Every time I double up the recipe and make her two loaves—one with walnuts and one with roll oats. Sometimes I replace half of the all-purpose flour with whole wheat flour to sneak in a little fiber without my kids knowing. I mean, you gotta love banana bread, because it makes you love better.

Mini Butter Honey
Whole Wheat Bread Loaves

• Makes 4 mini loaves •

No one will say no to a lovely loaf of bread. Lightly sweetened with honey, enriched with butter, and loaded with whole wheat, these loaves make wonderful sandwiches and toasts.

1 cup milk, warm (110°F)
¼ cup honey
2¼ tsp. active dry yeast
2½ cups whole wheat flour

1 tsp. salt
¼ cup unsalted butter, softened and cut
   into small pieces

Mini Butter Honey
Whole Wheat Bread Loaves

1. In the bowl of a standing mixer fitted with a paddle attachment, mix together the warm milk and honey. Sprinkle the yeast over the mixture. Let sit for 10 minutes.

2. Mix in the flour and salt until incorporated.

3. Slowly mix in the butter pieces.

4. Let the mixer knead the dough until it becomes very stretchy and sticky, about 5 minutes.

5. Place the dough in a lightly oiled large bowl. Cover and let rise for an hour.

6. Divide and place the dough pieces in four greased mini loaf pans. Cover and let dough rise for another hour.

7. Preheat oven to 350°F. Bake the loaves for 30 to 35 minutes, until golden brown.

8. Let cool completely.

Add Some Love...

Make them even healthier by adding roll oats, flax seeds, rye flour, millet, barley, etc.

Pumpkin and Cream Cheese Muffins with Walnut Streusel

• Makes 12 muffins •

Crunchy and nutty streusel, creamy cream cheese filling, and moist and spiced cakey muffins—these muffins are delicious and very addictive. Imagine a pumpkin cake in a muffin form for breakfast!

Cream Cheese Filling

½ cup cream cheese, softened
¼ cup granulated sugar
1 tsp. vanilla extract

Walnut Streusel

1/3 cup granulated sugar
½ cup flour
¼ cup walnuts, chopped
3 Tbsp. unsalted butter, melted

Pumpkin Muffins

2 cups flour
1½ cups granulated sugar
1 tsp. baking powder
1 tsp. baking soda
½ tsp. salt
1 tsp. ground cinnamon
1 tsp. ground ginger
½ tsp. ground nutmeg
1¼ cups pumpkin purée
3 large eggs, room temperature
1/3 cup vegetable oil

Cream Cheese Filling

1. Mix together all the ingredients until smooth. Refrigerate until ready to use.

Walnut Streusel

1. Mix together all the ingredients until the mixture resembles coarse sand.

Pumpkin Muffins

1. Preheat oven to 350°F. Line a muffin pan with liners.

2. In a large bowl, whisk together the flour, sugar, baking powder, baking soda, salt, cinnamon, ginger, and nutmeg.

3. In another large bowl, whisk the pumpkin purée, eggs, and oil until combined.

4. Mix in flour mixture until just incorporated.

5. Evenly divide half of the batter among the prepared muffin cups. Place 2 teaspoons of the cream cheese filling in the centre of each cup. Fill with the remaining batter.

6. Sprinkle 1 tablespoon of the streusel on top of each muffin.

7. Bake the muffins for 20 to 25 minutes, until the tops are golden brown.

8. Let cool completely.

Add Some Love...

Replace that coffee shop run with these bakery-worthy muffins. Just get busy in the kitchen, and create something special for your loved ones right here at home!

Apple Fritter Monkey Bread

• Makes an 8-inch round bread •

Monkey? Monkey bread? I have no idea about the name neither. Trust me, I did try to dig deep for the name source. But no one seems to care about it more than the making and eating of this sweet, sticky, and gooey goodness! This pull-apart bread tastes just like apple fritters. The little dough balls, coated with cinnamon sugar and caramel, are conveniently perfect for bite-size treats, something that you will pop in your mouth ALL DAY LONG!

Dough

6 Tbsp. warm water
¼ cup and 1 tsp. sugar
1½ tsp. active dry yeast
2¾ cups flour
6 Tbsp. sour cream, room temperature
¼ cup unsalted butter, softened
1 large egg, room temperature
1 tsp. salt
1 tsp. vanilla extract

Caramel Apple Filling

½ cup granulated sugar
2 Tbsp. water
3 Tbsp. unsalted butter
¼ cup heavy whipping cream
1 apple, peeled and cut into small pieces

Cinnamon Sugar Coating

1 cup granulated sugar
2 tsp. ground cinnamon
¼ cup unsalted butter, melted

Dough

1. In the bowl of a standing mixer fitted with a paddle attachment, mix together the water, teaspoon of sugar, yeast, and ¼ cup of the flour. Let sit for 10 minutes.

2. Mix in the sour cream, butter, egg, salt, and vanilla until combined.

3. Mix in the remaining flour until the mixture becomes a shaggy dough.

4. Switch to the dough hook. Knead the dough until it becomes soft and smooth, about 5 minutes.

5. Place the dough in a lightly oiled large bowl. Cover and let rise for 2 hours.

Apple Fritter Monkey Bread
(continued)

Caramel Apple Filling

1. Cook the sugar and water on low heat until the sugar is dissolved.

2. Add the butter. Let it come to a boil and cook until the mixture reaches a golden caramel color.

3. Remove from the heat. Whisk in the cream slowly.

Cinnamon Sugar Coating

1. Mix together the sugar and cinnamon in a small bowl.

2. Place the melted butter in another small bowl.

Add Some Love...

It's the perfect treat to make with kids on a snowy winter weekend. Get them involved in rolling the dough pieces into the balls, and building the bread in the pan. Your little bakers will be overjoyed with chipping in and nibbling the delicious treat.

Assemble: Gently deflate the dough. Shape it into 40 balls.

Pour half of the caramel into the prepared pan. Scatter half of the apples over the caramel.

Working one at a time, dip the dough balls in the melted butter, and then roll them in the cinnamon sugar.

Place 20 balls in the pan.

Top with the remaining caramel and apples. Continue dipping and placing the remaining dough balls in the pan.

Cover and let rise for another hour.

Preheat oven to 350°F. Bake the bread for 30 to 35 minutes, until the caramel begins to bubble around the edges, and the top is golden brown.

Let cool in pan for 10 minutes. Invert the bread, and let cool to room temperature.

Cranberry Cinnamon Rolls

• Makes 20 rolls •

My kids' first taste of cinnamon rolls was from Ikea many years ago. And that's when I decided to make my own, because you know homemade everything is always the best. Don't get intimidated, parents! This recipe is amazingly easy to work with. Instead of the normal two-time rising process, there is only one for these rolls, thanks to the use of yeast, baking powder, and baking soda together. At least once a week, my kids come home from school to the enticing smell of the freshly baked cinnamon rolls. And they cheer, "You are the best mama in the world!"

Filling

¼ cup unsalted butter, melted
1 tsp. ground cinnamon
1 cup light brown sugar
1 cup frozen cranberries

Dough

2 cups milk, warm (110°F)
½ cup vegetable oil
½ cup granulated sugar

2¼ tsp. active dry yeast
4½ cups flour
2 tsp. baking powder
2 tsp. baking soda
1 tsp. salt

Glaze

2 cups powdered sugar
1/3 cup heavy whipping cream
4 Tbsp. unsalted butter, melted

Filling

1. In a food processor, mix together the cinnamon, sugar, and cranberries until the mixture resembles wet sand.

Dough

1. Grease an 8-inch cake pan or cast-iron skillet.

2. Mix together the milk, oil, and sugar. Sprinkle the yeast over the mixture. Let sit for 10 minutes.

3. Mix in the flour, baking powder, baking soda, and salt until the mixture becomes very sticky.

4. On a well-floured surface, knead the dough until a smooth ball forms, about 5 minutes.

5. Flatten and roll the dough into a 20x28-inch rectangle. Brush the dough evenly with the melted butter. Sprinkle the filling on top.

6. Beginning with the long side, roll the dough into a log. Pinch the seam together at the end.

7. Cut the log into 20 equal slices. Place the sliced rolls in the prepared baking pans, one inch apart. Cover and let rise for 30 minutes.

8. Preheat oven to 350°F. Bake the rolls for 15 to 20 minutes, until golden brown.

Glaze

1. Whisk together all the ingredients until the mixture becomes thick and smooth. Generously drizzle the glaze over the hot rolls.

Add Some Love...

Want some freshly baked cinnamon rolls on a Saturday morning? Prepare and slice the dough the night before, then cover and refrigerate it without letting it rise. The next morning, remove the dough from the refrigerator and let it rise and bake while you are brushing teeth and making bed. You know your breakfast is ready when you smell that lovely cinnamon fragrance.

Double Chocolate Raspberry Muffins

• Makes 12 muffins •

These chocolatey and fruity muffins will become your favorite breakfast option. Each muffin is moist, tender, and loaded with chocolate chunks and tart raspberries. Are we talking about breakfast or dessert?

1 cup flour
¼ cup cocoa powder, sifted
1 cup granulated sugar
1 tsp. baking powder
1 tsp. baking soda
½ tsp. salt
1 large egg, room temperature

½ cup sour cream, room temperature
¼ cup vegetable oil
1 Tbsp. vanilla extract
½ cup hot water
½ cup dark chocolate chunks
1 cup raspberries

Double Chocolate Raspberry Muffins

1. Preheat oven to 350°F. Line a muffin pan with liners.

2. Whisk together the flour, cocoa powder, sugar, baking powder, baking soda, and salt.

3. Stir in the egg, sour cream, oil, and vanilla until combined.

4. Mix in the hot water slowly until the mixture becomes smooth.

5. Gently fold in half of the chocolate chunks and raspberries.

6. Evenly divide the batter among the prepared muffin cups, about halfway full. Place the remaining raspberries on top of the muffins.

7. Bake the muffins for 15 to 18 minutes, until a toothpick inserted in the muffin comes out clean. Let cool completely.

8. Microwave the remaining chocolate chunks until melted, stirring occasionally. Drizzle the melted chocolate over the muffins. Let set for 15 minutes.

Add Some Love...

This foolproof one-bowl recipe requires a little tender loving care. Mix until the dry ingredients are just incorporated. Do not over-mix the batter. It's perfectly fine to have some streaks of dry ingredients in the batter.

Brown Butter Maple Soda Bread

• Makes one loaf •

Bread lovers, this is your go-to recipe! Whipping up the batter only takes a few minutes. The bread is tender, incredibly buttery, and naturally sweet. No traditional white bread can compare with this soda bread.

¼ cup unsalted butter
3 cups flour
1 Tbsp. baking powder
½ Tbsp. baking soda

2 Tbsp. granulated sugar
1 tsp. salt
2 Tbsp. maple syrup
1½ cups buttermilk, room temperature

Brown Butter Maple Soda Bread

1. Preheat oven to 350°F. Grease and line a loaf pan with parchment paper.

2. Cook the butter on medium heat until it turns brown and smells nutty, about 10 minutes, stirring occasionally and skimming the foam as necessary. Remove from heat. Let cool to room temperature.

3. In a large bowl, mix together the flour, baking powder, baking soda, sugar, and salt.

4. Mix in the maple syrup and buttermilk until just incorporated.

5. Pour half of the melted butter into the loaf pan. Then pour the batter over the melted butter, followed by the rest of the melted butter on top of the batter.

6. Bake 55 to 60 minutes, until the top is golden brown and a toothpick inserted in the bread center comes out clean.

7. Let the bread cool in pan for 10 minutes. Remove from pan and let cool to room temperature.

Add Some Love...

The best time to make this bread is soup season. A nice thick slice of bread will definitely elevate the enjoyment of many soups. But it's also good anytime you are craving some carbs.

Granola with Almonds, Dried Cranberries, and Coconut

• Makes 10 cups •

Such a granola monster family, we always have a jar or two of homemade granola in our kitchen pantry. Dump it over yogurt for breakfast, grab a handful for a snack after school, sprinkle some on ice cream for dessert. . . . Homemade granola is always cheaper, healthier, and tastier compared to the store-bought ones. It also makes the perfect edible gift, as it allows you to get personal and creative with the packaging, ingredients, and flavors.

½ cup coconut oil, melted
½ cup maple syrup
1 Tbsp. vanilla extract
1 tsp. salt

6 cups rolled oats
2 cups whole almonds, roughly chopped
1 cup dried cranberries
1 cup unsweetened coconut flakes

Granola with Almonds, Dried Cranberries, and Coconut

1. Preheat oven to 300°F. Line two cookie sheet pans with parchment paper.

2. Whisk together the coconut oil, maple syrup, vanilla, and salt until combined.

3. Fold in the oats and almonds until completely coated.

4. Spread the mixture in an even layer on each of the prepared pans.

5. Bake until crispy and toasted, 40 to 45 minutes. Stir once halfway through.

6. Let cool completely.

7. Stir in dried cranberries and coconut.

Add Some Love...

Making granola requires no rules. Anything works! You are looking for a nice mix of saltiness, sweetness, and crunchiness. My daughter always asks for some candies in her granola, and you know what, chocolate chips work just fine!

Lemon Blueberry Dutch Baby Pancakes

• Makes a 10-inch pancake •

Five minutes tops is what you need to whip up this baby! Put it in the oven, prepare the toppings, and you have an amazingly beautiful and delicious pancake breakfast. By using just eggs, milk, flour, and butter, you can instantly create a magical golden puffy goodness!

3 large eggs
1/3 cup milk
½ cup flour
½ tsp. vanilla extract
¼ tsp. salt

3 Tbsp. butter
1 cup lemon curd (recipe on page 15)
1 cup fresh blueberries
1 Tbsp. powdered sugar

Lemon Blueberry Dutch Baby Pancakes

1. Preheat oven to 425°F.

2. In a food processor, blend together the eggs, milk, flour, vanilla, and salt until smooth.

3. Melt the butter in a large cast-iron skillet on high heat until bubbling. Pour the egg mixture over the melted butter.

4. Bake 15 to 20 minutes, until the pancake is puffed and golden brown.

5. Top the pancake with lemon curd and blueberries.

6. Sprinkle with powdered sugar.

Add Some Love...

Make two pancakes to cure the sweet tooth and also cater the savoury craving. Top the savory one with eggs, bacon, cheese, mushrooms. . . . Everyone is happy!

Raspberry Almond Scones

• Makes 8 scones •

Pass the butter, please! Tender and flaky scones are calling! A perfect holiday brunch doesn't have to be fancy. Here come buttery and melt-in-your-mouth scones that even a first-time baker can attempt and walk away with an impressive product! These scones come together with minimal ingredients. The addition of raspberries and almonds simply turns the everyday pastry into something special for the holidays!

2 cups flour
1 Tbsp. baking powder
1 tsp. salt
¼ cup granulated sugar
1 cup unsalted butter, cut into little pieces and chilled

1 large egg
¼ cup buttermilk
½ cup fresh raspberries
¼ cup sliced almonds

Raspberry Almond Scones

1. Preheat oven to 350°F. Line two cookie sheet pans with parchment paper.

2. In a large bowl, whisk together the flour, baking powder, salt, and sugar.

3. Use a pastry cutter to cut butter pieces in the flour mixture until it resembles coarse sand.

4. In a small bowl, mix together the egg and buttermilk until combined. Reserve 2 tablespoons for egg wash.

5. Stir the egg mixture in the flour mixture until the dough comes together. Fold in the raspberries.

6. On a well-floured surface, knead the dough until it becomes soft and smooth.

7. Flatten the dough to two inches thick. Use a 3-inch floured cookie cutter to cut out the scones. Place them on the prepared pans. Brush the tops with the reserved egg mixture. Sprinkle the almonds on top.

8. Bake the scones for 15 to 20 minutes, until the tops are golden brown.

Add Some Love...

A general rule for making delicate scones is to keep everything cold and work the dough as little as possible. Simply work quickly!

Lemon Pistachio Muffins

• Makes 15 muffins •

*Big on flavor but light on texture, these muffins are moist, tender, and bursting
with bright lemon flavor. The pistachios give the perfect nutty crunch bonus.
Don't skip that lemon glaze! It really takes the muffins up a citrus notch!*

Lemon Pistachio Muffins

2 cups flour
¾ cup granulated sugar
1 tsp. baking powder
1 tsp. baking soda
½ tsp. salt
2 large eggs, room temperature
1 cup milk, room temperature

½ cup unsalted butter, melted and cooled
1 Tbsp. lemon zest
¼ cup lemon juice
½ cup pistachios, roughly chopped

Lemon Glaze

1 cup powdered sugar
2–3 Tbsp. lemon juice
¼ cup pistachio, roughly chopped

Lemon Pistachio Muffins

1. Preheat oven to 350°F. Line two muffin pans with liners.

2. In a large bowl, whisk together the flour, sugar, baking powder, baking soda, and salt.

3. In another large bowl, whisk together the eggs, milk, melted butter, lemon zest, and juice.

4. Stir in the flour mixture until just incorporated. Fold in the pistachios.

5. Evenly divide the batter among the prepared muffin cups.

6. Bake 15 to 20 minutes, until a toothpick inserted in the muffin comes out clean.

7. Let cool completely.

Lemon Glaze

1. Whisk together the sugar and lemon juice until slightly thickened and pourable.

2. Spoon the glaze over the muffins. Sprinkle the pistachios on top.

Add Some Love...

The muffins are fine plain, or simply dusted with powdered sugar. In fact, you can easily turn them into pretty cupcakes by topping with icing. I'm thinking lemon cream cheese frosting (recipe on page 154).

It's time to turn on the oven; get out the flour, butter, sugar, and spices; peel and dice fresh seasonal fruits; and turn all of these ingredients into a glorious homemade pie. From tart and fruity pie, such as red berry pie and blueberry peach ginger pie, to luscious and elegant-looking cranberry lime shortbread tart and pumpkin chiffon tart, these recipes share a wealth of inspirations for producing something more impressive than a traditional pumpkin pie. Ditch that double crust blanket and jazz up your pie presentation with some easy dough cut-out shapes or letters. The step-by-step lattice pie top tutorial will definitely help weave your way to success.

Pies | Tarts

Cranberry Lime Shortbread Tart

• Makes a 9-inch tart •

Feast your eyes with the natural vibrant scarlet color before the brightly intense tart-sweetness and velvety texture hit your tongue. This cranberry lime shortbread tart is an absolute show-stopper on your dessert table. Perfectly balanced, silky smooth, and insatiably delicious!

Vanilla Shortbread Crust

½ cup unsalted butter
¼ cup powdered sugar
½ Tbsp. vanilla extract
1 cup flour
¼ tsp. salt

Cranberry Lime Curd

4 cups cranberries, fresh or frozen
1 cup granulated sugar
½ cup lime juice
2 tsp. lime zest
½ cup water
4 egg yolks
1 Tbsp. cornstarch
2 Tbsp. unsalted butter

Whipped Cream Topping

½ cup heavy whipping cream
1 Tbsp. powdered sugar
¼ cup fresh cranberries
1 tsp. lime zest

Vanilla Shortbread Crust

1. Grease a 9-inch tart pan with a removable bottom.

2. In the bowl of a standing mixer fitted with a paddle attachment, beat the butter and powdered sugar on medium speed until light and fluffy, about 5 minutes.

3. Mix in the vanilla until combined.

4. Sift in the flour and salt. Mix on low speed until just incorporated.

5. Press the mixture onto the bottom and sides of the prepared pan.

6. Freeze the crust for 10 minutes.

7. Preheat oven to 350°F. Bake the crust for 15 to 20 minutes. Let cool completely.

Cranberry Lime Shortbread Tart
(continued)

Cranberry Lime Curd

1. Cook the cranberries, ½ cup sugar, lime juice, lime zest, and water on medium heat for 10 minutes, stirring occasionally, until the cranberries are popped and release their juice.

2. Pulse the mixture in a food processor.

3. Blend in the egg yolks, remaining sugar, and cornstarch until combined.

4. Cook the mixture again on low heat while whisking for 10 minutes until thickened.

5. Remove from heat. Mix in the butter until combined.

6. Strain the mixture to make it smooth.

7. Let cool to room temperature.

8. Fill the cooled crust with the cranberry lime curd.

9. Refrigerate the tart until set, at least 4 hours.

Whipped Cream Topping

1. Whisk the cream and sugar until firm peaks form. Transfer the whipped cream to a piping bag with a star tip.

2. Remove the tart from the pan.

3. Pipe the whipped cream along the edges of the tart.

4. Top with cranberries and lime zest.

Add Some Love...

You don't have to do much for this tart, thanks to its gorgeous color, but you can always treat yourself better by planning ahead for your big celebration day. The curd can be made five days in advance and kept refrigerated with a plastic wrap covered directly on the surface to avoid a skin forming.

Mini Toffee Apple Pies

• Makes six 4-inch pies •

Good things come in small packages, and when it comes to mini pies, it's definitely true. They are convenient in big gatherings—no slicing is required. And they look spectacular on the dessert table. If you find making a full pie too intimidating, get started with the mini ones. You can easily achieve an amazing result with just a fraction of the work.

Pastry Pie Crusts

1¼ cups flour
½ Tbsp. granulated sugar
½ tsp. salt
½ cup unsalted butter, cut into little pieces, chilled
4–6 Tbsp. cold water
1 egg yolk
1 Tbsp. water

Toffee Apple Filling

6 Granny Smith apples, peeled, cored, and sliced
4 Tbsp. unsalted butter
1 cup brown sugar
4 Tbsp. salted caramel (recipe on page 16)
1 ground cinnamon

Egg Wash

1 egg yolk
1 Tbsp. water

Pastry Pie Crusts

1. In a food processor, mix the flour, sugar, and salt.

2. Scatter the butter pieces over the flour mixture. Pulse until the mixture resembles coarse sand.

3. Add 4 tablespoons water, and pulse the dough. Add more water, a tablespoon at a time, until the dough holds together when pinched.

4. Gather and form a dough. Cover dough with plastic wrap and refrigerate for 30 minutes.

5. Grease six 4-inch tartlet pans.

6. On a lightly floured surface, roll out the dough to ¼-inch thickness. Cut into six 5-inch rounds. Line the prepared pans with the dough rounds. Use a small fork to poke holes on the bottom of each dough.

7. Cut the remaining dough into ½-inch-wide strips.

8. Refrigerate the doughs and strips for 10 minutes.

Toffee Apple Filling

1. Cook the apples, butter, sugar, and salted caramel in a saucepan on medium heat for about 10 minutes, stirring occasionally, until the apples are soft and almost fall apart.

2. Let cool to room temperature.

Assemble and Bake

1. Preheat oven to 375°F. Evenly fill the pie crusts with the filling.

2. Place three or four strips over the filling, evenly spaced, and then weave with the remaining strips diagonally. Adhere the ends to the edges of the crusts.

3. Mix together the egg yolk and water. Brush the egg wash over the pie crusts.

4. Bake the pies for 20 to 25 minutes, until the tops of the pie crusts are golden brown.

5. Let cool for 30 minutes before removing the pies from the pans.

Add Some Love...

Don't forget that big pint of vanilla ice cream!

Chocolate Cream Hazelnut Tart

• Makes a 9-inch tart •

Silky smooth consistency, pronounced chocolate flavor, buttery hazelnut shortbread crust, and whipped cream topping—this heavenly chocolate cream hazelnut tart will move you through Thanksgiving and into the Christmas season as well.

Hazelnut Shortbread Crust

½ cup unsalted butter
¼ cup powdered sugar
½ Tbsp. vanilla extract
¼ cup hazelnuts, finely chopped
1 cup flour
¼ tsp. salt

Chocolate Cream Filling

½ cup granulated sugar
2 large eggs, lightly beaten

70 grams dark chocolate
½ cup unsalted butter, softened
¾ cup heavy whipping cream

Chocolate Whipped Cream Topping

1 cup heavy whipping cream
2 Tbsp. cocoa powder
2 Tbsp. powdered sugar
¼ cup hazelnut halves, lightly toasted

Hazelnut Shortbread Crust

1. Grease a 9-inch tart pan with a removable bottom.

2. In the bowl of a standing mixer fitted with a paddle attachment, beat the butter and powdered sugar on medium speed until light and fluffy, about 5 minutes.

3. Mix in the vanilla until combined.

4. Add the hazelnuts. Sift in the flour and salt. Mix on low speed until just incorporated.

5. Press the mixture onto the bottom and sides of the prepared pan.

6. Freeze the crust for 10 minutes.

7. Preheat oven to 350°F. Bake the crust for 15 to 20 minutes. Let cool completely.

Chocolate Cream Hazelnut Tart
(continued)

Chocolate Cream Filling

1. Set a small bowl over a pan of simmering water. Whisk the sugar and eggs until the mixture is thick enough to coat the back of a spoon, about 5 minutes.

2. Stir in the chocolate until melted and combined.

3. Remove from heat. Let cool completely.

4. In the bowl of a standing mixer fitted with a paddle attachment, beat the butter until light and fluffy.

5. Beat in the cooled chocolate mixture until combined.

6. In another bowl, whip the cream until firm peaks form.

7. Fold the whipped cream into the chocolate mixture until the cream is incorporated and the mixture is light and fluffy.

8. Pour the mixture in the cooled tart shell. Smooth the top.

9. Refrigerate the tart until set, at least 4 hours.

Chocolate Whipped Cream Topping

1. Whisk the cream, cocoa powder, and sugar until firm peaks form. Transfer the whipped cream to a piping bag with a star tip.

2. Remove the tart from the pan.

3. Pipe the whipped cream on top of the tart.

4. Sprinkle the toasted hazelnuts on top.

> ### Add Some Love...
>
> Love the combination of chocolate and orange? You can easily convert this tart into a chocolate orange tart by adding a tablespoon of orange zest each to the crust and filling.

Peach Blueberry Ginger Pie

• Makes a 9-inch pie •

Pie is love and comfort on a plate. There's something very satisfying about biting into a crispy pastry case to meet the warm, soft filling. The combination of melting gooey syrup and buttery flaky pie crust is pure pleasure. This peach and blueberry pie is your answer to that plain old apple pie. The sweet and juicy fruits bring memories of summertime, but the spicy fresh ginger and cinnamon bring a welcoming warmth to the pie. It tastes like summer. It takes like autumn. It tastes like Grandma's. It tastes like pure love.

Pastry Pie Crust

2½ cups flour

1 Tbsp. granulated sugar

1 tsp. salt

1 cup unsalted butter, cut into little pieces, chilled

6–8 Tbsp. cold water

Ginger, Peach, and Blueberry Filling

¼ cup flour

1 Tbsp. cornstarch

1/3 cup granulated sugar

½ tsp. ground cinnamon

4 cups sliced peaches, fresh or frozen

1 cup blueberries, fresh or frozen

1 Tbsp. lemon juice

1 tsp. freshly grated ginger

Egg Wash

1 egg yolk

1 Tbsp. water

Pastry Pie Crust

1. In a food processor, mix the flour, sugar, and salt.

2. Scatter the butter pieces over the flour mixture. Pulse until the mixture resembles coarse sand.

3. Add 6 tablespoons water and pulse the dough. Add more water, a tablespoon at a time, until the dough holds together when pinched with fingers.

4. Gather and form two doughs. Cover both with plastic wrap, and refrigerate for 30 minutes.

5. Grease a 9-inch pie pan.

6. On a lightly floured surface, roll out one of the doughs to ¼-inch thickness. Line the prepared pan with the dough. Use a small fork to poke holes on the bottom of the dough.

7. Refrigerate the dough for 10 minutes.

Peach Blueberry Ginger Pie
(continued)

Ginger, Peach, and Blueberry Filling

1. Whisk together the flour, cornstarch, sugar, and cinnamon.

2. Toss in the peaches, blueberries, lemon juice, and ginger until the fruits are well coated with the flour mixture.

3. Let sit for 30 minutes.

Add Some Love...

I like to overfill my pie with love by adorning it with more than a top crust covering. Weave a lattice, make a braided edge, or top with cut-out letters . . . the possibilities are endless.

Assemble and Bake

1. Preheat the oven to 375°F. Pour the filling in the pie crust.

2. Roll out the remaining dough to ¼-inch thickness. Drape it over the filling. Crimp dough evenly around the edges of the pan using a fork.

3. Slash the top crust several times to vent the steam when baking.

4. Mix together the egg yolk and water. Brush the egg wash over the pie crust.

5. Bake the pie for 50 to 55 minutes, until the top of the pie crust is golden brown.

6. Let cool for at least an hour before serving.

Weave the Perfect Lattice Pie Crust

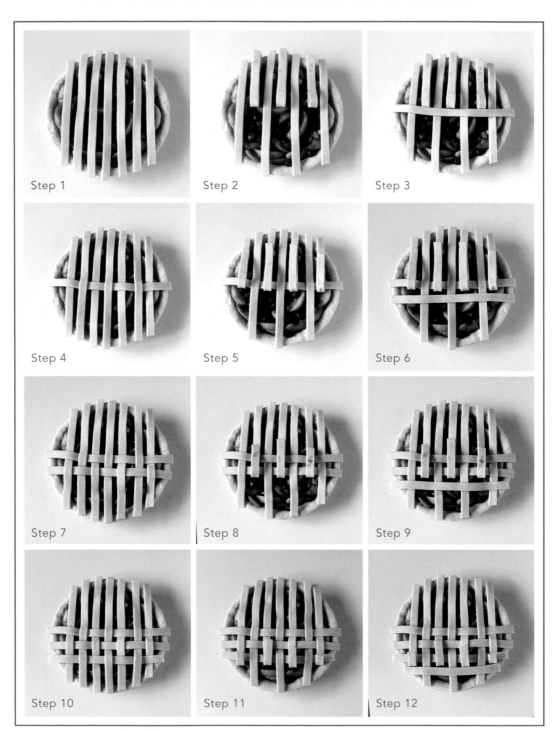

Step 1

Step 2

Step 3

Step 4

Step 5

Step 6

Step 7

Step 8

Step 9

Step 10

Step 11

Step 12

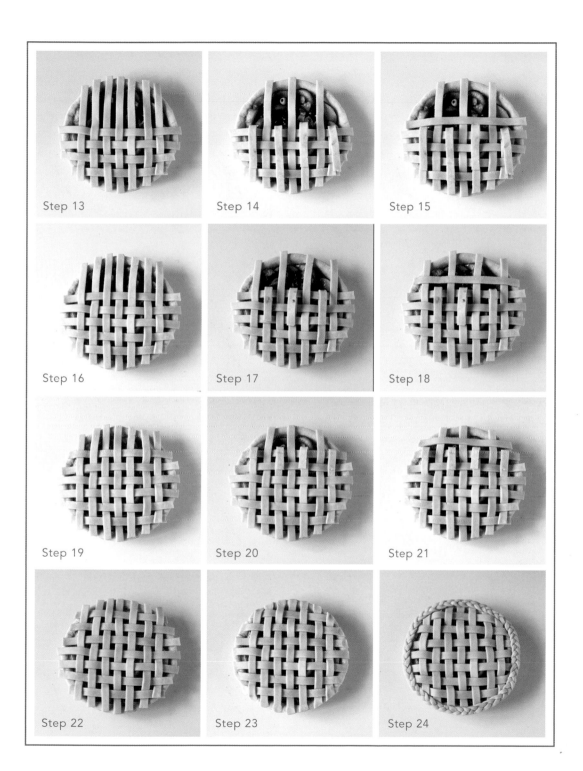

Step 13

Step 14

Step 15

Step 16

Step 17

Step 18

Step 19

Step 20

Step 21

Step 22

Step 23

Step 24

Red Berry Pie

• Makes a 9-inch pie or two 7-inch pies •

Jewel-toned berries team up to pack this pretty pie with festive color and flavor. The natural tartness from cranberries pairs so well with the sweetness of raspberries and strawberries. When cooked together, the berries pop and break down so you end up with a glistening red sauce full of berry goodness! And how pleasing it is to personalize the pie dough pattern. As simple as using some cookie cutters or just a knife, you are ready to have fun making food that is not only delicious but also exciting and memorable.

Pastry Pie Crust

2½ cups flour
1 Tbsp. granulated sugar
1 tsp. salt
1 cup unsalted butter, cut into little pieces, chilled
6–8 Tbsp. cold water

Egg Wash

1 egg yolk
1 Tbsp. water

Cranberry, Strawberry, and Raspberry Filling

3 cups cranberries, fresh or frozen
1½ cups strawberries, fresh or frozen
1½ cups raspberries, fresh or frozen
1 cup granulated sugar
3 Tbsp. cornstarch
1 tsp. ground cinnamon
1 Tbsp. water

Pastry Pie Crust

1. In a food processor, mix the flour, sugar, and salt.

2. Scatter the butter pieces over the flour mixture. Pulse until the mixture resembles coarse sand.

3. Add 6 tablespoons water, and pulse the dough. Add more water, a tablespoon at a time, until the dough holds together when pinched.

4. Gather and form two doughs. Cover both with plastic wrap and refrigerate for 30 minutes.

5. Grease a 9-inch pie pan.

6. On a lightly floured surface, roll out one of the doughs to ¼-inch thickness. Line the prepared pan with the dough. Use a small fork to poke holes on the bottom of dough.

7. Roll out another dough. Cut out your preferred shapes with floured cookie cutters.

8. Refrigerate the dough and dough cut-outs for 10 minutes.

Cranberries, Strawberry, and Raspberry Filling

1. Cook all the ingredients on medium heat for about 10 minutes, stirring occasionally, until the berries are soft and the mixture is thickened.

2. Let cool to room temperature.

Assemble and Bake: Preheat oven to 375°F. Pour the filling in the pie crust. Carefully place the dough cut-outs over the filling.

Whisk together the egg yolk and water. Brush the egg wash over the pie crust.

Bake the pie for 50 to 55 minutes, until the top of the pie crust is golden brown. For smaller pies, cut down the baking time to 40 to 45 minutes.

Let cool for at least an hour before serving.

Add Some Love...

My favorite pie decoration is "message in a pie," one that gives a personal touch with a fun and caring message. Use alphabet cookie cutters to cut out "I love you," "Happy New Year," or "Let's be friends," and place the message on your pie before baking.

Oh Sweet Day!'s
Famous Shortbread Tartlets

• Makes twelve 3-inch tartlets •

*What's better than shortbread cookies? I would have to say shortbread tartlets.
The overflowing love for my shortbread cookies got my brain ticking, and I came up with
something even more irresistible. These tender, crisp, buttery shortbread shells are filled with an
assortment of scrumptious and vibrant-looking fillings. I like to tell my customers at the
farmer's markets, "If you like shortbread, these shortbread tartlets are going to be very dangerous!"*

Vanilla Shortbread Crusts

1 cup unsalted butter, softened
½ cup powdered sugar
1 Tbsp. vanilla extract
2 cups flour
½ tsp. salt

Chocolate Shortbread Crusts

2 Tbsp. cocoa powder, sifted

Salted Caramel Filling

½ cup granulated sugar
2 Tbsp. water
3 Tbsp. unsalted butter
¼ cup heavy whipping cream
2 tsp. sea salt flakes

Roasted Strawberry Filling

2 cups fresh or frozen strawberries
¼ cup granulated sugar
1 Tbsp. balsamic vinegar

Chocolate Ganache Filling

2/3 cup heavy whipping cream
200 grams dark chocolate, cut into small
    pieces

Lemon Curd Filling

¾ cup lemon juice
1 Tbsp. lemon zest
¾ cup granulated sugar
3 large eggs
½ cup unsalted butter

Peach Blueberry Ginger Filling

2 cups sliced peaches
¼ cup granulated sugar
1 Tbsp. cornstarch
1 tsp. freshly grated ginger
¼ cup fresh blueberries

Oh Sweet Day!'s
Famous Shortbread Tartlets
(continued)

Vanilla Shortbread Crusts

1. In the bowl of a standing mixer fitted with a paddle attachment, beat the butter and powdered sugar on medium speed until light and fluffy, about 5 minutes.

2. Mix in the vanilla until combined.

3. Sift in the flour and salt. Mix on low speed until just incorporated.

4. Gather and form a dough. Cover with plastic wrap and refrigerate for 30 minutes.

5. Preheat oven to 350°F. Grease twelve 3-inch tartlet pans or two jumbo-sized muffin pans.

6. On a lightly floured surface, roll out the dough to ¼-inch thickness. Cut into 4-inch rounds. Line the prepared pans with the dough rounds.

7. Freeze the crusts for 10 minutes.

8. Bake the crusts for 10 to 15 minutes. Let cool completely. Invert the crusts.

Chocolate Shortbread Crusts

1. Follow above instructions, but sift in the cocoa powder with the flour and salt.

Salted Caramel Filling

1. Cook the sugar and water on low heat until the sugar is dissolved.

2. Add the butter. Let it come to a boil and cook until the mixture reaches a golden caramel color.

3. Remove from the heat. Whisk in the cream slowly. Mix in a teaspoon of sea salt.

4. Let cool to room temperature.

Roasted Strawberry Filling

1. Preheat oven to 350°F.

2. In an 8-inch square baking pan, mix all the ingredients until the strawberries are well coated with sugar.

3. Spread the mixture in a single layer. Roast the strawberries for an hour. Stir once, halfway through.

4. Mash the mixture with a fork. Let cool completely.

Chocolate Ganache Filling

1. Microwave the cream on high for 45 seconds.

2. Pour the hot cream over the chocolate. Let sit for a minute, then whisk together until smooth.

3. Let cool slightly.

Lemon Curd Filling

1. Cook the lemon juice, zest, sugar, and eggs on low heat while whisking for 10 minutes until thickened.

2. Remove from heat. Mix in the butter until combined.

3. Strain the lemon curd to make it smooth.

4. Let cool to room temperature.

Peach Blueberry Ginger Filling

1. Cook the peaches, sugar, cornstarch, and ginger on medium heat for 5 minutes, stirring occasionally, until thickened.

2. Let cool to room temperature.

3. Gently stir in the blueberries.

Assemble: Fill each of the cooled shell with ¼ cup filling.

Add Some Love...

The tartlets look extra pretty when studded with fresh fruits, mint leaves, lemon rinds, sea salt flakes, chocolate shavings. To make your life easier, you can make and freeze the baked tartlet shells and the fillings up to a week in advance. Thaw everything at room temperature and assemble the day before you serve them.

Pumpkin Chiffon Tart

• Makes a 9-inch tart •

Who doesn't love a good pumpkin pie? But what if you get to point when you are so full from the holiday dinner, and all you want for dessert is something just as delicious but a little lighter? This pumpkin chiffon tart is your answer! A silkier and prettier version of the traditional pumpkin dessert, this tart is so fluffy and delicate. You will have a hard time resisting the second or third slice.

Graham Cracker Crust

1½ cups graham cracker crumbs
¼ cup unsalted butter, melted

Pumpkin Filling

½ Tbsp. unflavored gelatin powder
2 Tbsp. water
1 cup pumpkin purée
3 Tbsp. brown sugar
½ tsp. ground cinnamon

½ tsp. ground ginger
¼ tsp. salt
¼ cup heavy whipping cream
2 large egg whites
2 Tbsp. granulated sugar

Whipped Cream Topping

1 cup heavy whipping cream
2 Tbsp. powdered sugar
¼ cup chopped pecans
¼ cup sunflower seeds

Graham Cracker Crust

1. Preheat oven to 350°F. Grease a 9-inch springform pan.

2. Mix all the ingredients together until the mixture resembles wet sand.

3. Firmly press the mixture into the bottom and sides of the prepared pan.

4. Bake 10 to 15 minutes, until the edges are golden brown.

5. Let cool completely.

Pumpkin Filling

1. Sprinkle the gelatin powder in water. Let sit for 5 minutes. Microwave 10 to 20 seconds on high until the gelatin dissolves. Let cool slightly.

2. In a food processor, blend the pumpkin, sugar, cinnamon, ginger, and salt until smooth.

3. Add the cream and gelatin mixture to the food processor. Pulse to combine.

4. In the bowl of a stand mixer with a whisk, beat the egg whites on medium speed until foamy.

5. Gradually add the sugar, and continue beating until firm peaks form.

6. Fold the meringue in the pumpkin mixture, half at a time, until just incorporated.

7. Pour the batter into the cooled crust. Smooth the top.

8. Refrigerate the tart until set, at least 4 hours.

Whipped Cream Topping

1. Whisk the cream and sugar until firm peaks form. Transfer the whipped cream to a piping bag with a star tip.

2. Pipe the whipped cream on top of the tart. Sprinkles the pecans and sunflower seeds on top.

Add Some Love...

Although it's fine to use canned pumpkin, the natural sweetness from Japanese pumpkins in this recipe helps cut down the sugar in the filling. Look for these green-skinned pumpkins; they are available all year, but they are best in late summer and early fall.

Strawberry Mascarpone Tartlets

• Makes eight 4-inch tartlets •

You can't have too many fruit tarts. The luxurious lemony mascarpone filling goes great with the fresh, bright-red, sweet strawberries. The addition of pistachios adds some crunch and a delightfully nutty flavor. The pastry crust, by the way, is a breeze to make.

Pastry Tartlet Crusts

1¼ cups all-purpose flour

½ Tbsp. granulated sugar

½ tsp. salt

½ cup unsalted butter, cut into little pieces, chilled

4–6 Tbsp. cold water

Strawberry Mascarpone Filling

¾ cup heavy whipping cream

1 cup mascarpone cheese

½ cup powdered sugar

1 Tbsp. lemon juice

Toppings

2 cups fresh strawberries, halved

½ cup pistachios, roughly chopped

Pastry Tartlet Crusts

1. In a food processor, mix the flour, sugar, and salt.

2. Scatter the butter pieces over the flour mixture. Pulse until the mixture resembles coarse sand.

3. Add 4 tablespoons water, and pulse the dough. Add more water, a tablespoon at a time, until the dough holds together when pinched with fingers.

4. Gather and form a dough. Cover with plastic wrap and refrigerate for 30 minutes.

5. Grease eight 4-inch tartlet pans.

6. On a lightly floured surface, roll out the dough to ¼-inch thickness. Cut into 5-inch rounds. Line the prepared pans with the dough rounds. Use a small fork to poke holes on the bottom of each crust.

7. Refrigerate the crusts for 10 minutes.

8. Preheat oven to 350°F. Bake the tartlets for 15 to 20 minutes.

9. Let the tartlet crusts cool completely. Invert the crusts.

Strawberry Mascarpone Filling

1. In the bowl of a standing mixer fitted with a whisk, beat the cream until it holds firm peaks. Transfer the whipped cream to another bowl and keep it in the refrigerator.

2. In the same bowl, using a paddle attachment, beat the mascarpone cheese, powdered sugar, and lemon juice until combined.

3. Fold in the whipped cream until incorporated.

Assemble: Fill the cooled shell with ¼ cup of the filling. Top with the strawberry halves and chopped pistachios.

Add Some Love...

Feel free to use other berries and nuts, like blueberries and walnuts, raspberries and hazelnuts, blackberries and almonds, and so on. The goal is to create the perfect balance of creaminess, fruitiness, and crunchiness. A little creativity will definitely take these tartlets to another level!

Be it a little bag of six or a fancy box of assorted ones, homemade cookies always bring the warmth and friendliness of your own kitchen to others. And who doesn't get excited about a freshly baked dozen? For a very small amount of time, you can easily whip up edible gifts that are guaranteed to make your loved ones smile. And if you want to make a test run for yourself, that's totally okay. I used to think that shortbread was only for the holidays, but my customers convinced me otherwise. I sell *Oh Sweet Day!*'s special flavored shortbread cookies all year around at farmer's markets because they are always delicious! And you know, any time you don't have a clue, shortbread is always the answer!

Cookies | Macarons

Oh Sweet Day!'s Famous Shortbread Cookies

• Makes 36 cookies •

*During the holiday season, my schedule is jam-packed with cookie gift box orders.
My oven never gets a chance to cool down as it bakes over ten thousand cookies, mostly my special
flavored shortbread. Putting* Oh Sweet Day! *on the map, this collection of shortbread cookies is one of the
customers' favorites at the farmer's markets. Shortbread is love, comfort, and memories. Shortbread is
the answer for everything. You are just a few basic ingredients away from delighting your loved ones.*

Classic Vanilla Shortbread

1 cup unsalted butter, softened
½ cup powdered sugar
1 Tbsp. vanilla extract
2 cups flour
½ tsp. salt

Lemon Lavender Shortbread

1 Tbsp. lemon zest
1 Tbsp. dried lavender

Dark Chocolate Shortbread

2 Tbsp. cocoa powder, sifted

Orange Hazelnut Shortbread

2 Tbsp. orange zest
¼ cup hazelnuts, finely chopped

Coconut Shortbread

¼ cup unsweetened coconut

Dried Cranberry and Pistachio Shortbread

¼ cup dried cranberries, chopped
¼ cup pistachios, finely chopped

Classic Vanilla Shortbread

1. In the bowl of a standing mixer fitted with a paddle attachment, beat the butter and powdered sugar on medium speed until light and fluffy, about 5 minutes.

2. Mix in the vanilla until combined.

3. Sift in the flour and salt. Mix on low speed until just incorporated.

4. Gather and form a dough. Cover with plastic wrap and refrigerate for 30 minutes.

5. Preheat oven to 325°F. Line two cookie sheet pans with parchment paper.

6. On a lightly floured surface, roll out the dough to ¼-inch thickness. Cut into rounds using a 2-inch floured cookie cutter. Place the cookies on the prepared baking pans.

7. Bake 15 to 18 minutes. Let cool completely.

Lemon Lavender Shortbread

1. Follow the directions for vanilla shortbread, but replace the vanilla with the lemon zest and dried lavender.

Dark Chocolate Shortbread

1. Follow the directions for vanilla shortbread, but sift in the cocoa powder with the flour and salt.

Orange Hazelnut Shortbread

1. Follow the directions for vanilla shortbread, but replace the vanilla with the orange zest. Add the hazelnuts with the flour and salt.

Coconut Shortbread

1. Follow the directions for vanilla shortbread, but add the coconut with the flour and salt.

Dried Cranberry and Pistachio Shortbread

1. Follow the directions for vanilla shortbread, but add the dried cranberries and pistachios with the flour and salt.

Add Some Love...

Take extra care when giving shortbread cookies away. They crumble very easily. You don't want them to break into pieces until they reach the mouths of their grateful recipients.

Blueberry Swirl Meringue Cookies

• Makes 20 cookies •

Almost too pretty to eat, these light and fluffy meringue cookies, slightly swirled a fresh blueberry syrup, take traditional meringues to a whole new level. You can easily customize the swirl pattern with different berries, chocolate, caramel, or whatever you'd like. You can also add a sprinkle of nuts for the extra crunch!

Blueberry Sauce

1 cup blueberries, fresh or frozen

3 Tbsp. granulated sugar

Meringue Cookies

3 large egg whites

1 tsp. lemon juice

½ tsp. cream of tartar

¾ cup granulated sugar

Blueberry Sauce

1. Cook the blueberries and sugar on medium heat until the blueberries are soft and release their juice, about 10 minutes.

2. Strain the sauce. Let cool completely.

Meringue Cookies

1. Preheat oven to 225°F. Line two cookie sheet pans with parchment paper.

2. In the bowl of a standing mixer fitted with a whisk, beat the egg whites, lemon juice, and cream of tartar on medium speed until foamy.

3. Reduce the speed to low and gradually add the sugar, a tablespoon at a time.

4. Increase the speed to high and beat until firm peaks form, about 5 minutes.

5. Spoon about 20 balls of meringue onto the prepared pans. Smooth the tops with the back of a spoon.

6. Drizzle about ½ teaspoon of the blueberry sauce on each meringue. Use a toothpick to swirl the sauce in the meringue.

7. Bake 80 to 90 minutes. Turn off the oven. Leave the cookies in the oven for 2 hours to finish drying.

Add Some Love...

These beautiful meringue cookies make the perfect dessert. Right before serving, top the cookies with a dollop of whipped cream, some fresh berries, and a sprinkle of powdered sugar.

Chocolate Nutella Sandwich Cookies

• Makes 20 sandwich cookies •

Sandwich cookies are special. You are literally eating two cookies at the same time, plus some delicious bonus in between. When it comes to buttery, chocolatey cookies paired with creamy chocolate-hazelnut filling that you can whip up in no time, these ultimate tasty treats are definitely the most winning edible gift.

1 cup unsalted butter, softened	½ tsp. salt
½ cup powdered sugar	1½ cups Nutella
2 cups flour	¼ cup dark chocolate chips
2 Tbsp. cocoa powder	

Chocolate Nutella Sandwich Cookies

1. In the bowl of a standing mixer fitted with a paddle attachment, beat the butter and sugar on medium speed until light and fluffy, about 5 minutes.

2. Sift in the flour, cocoa powder, and salt. Mix in low speed until just incorporated.

3. Gather and form a dough. Cover with plastic wrap and refrigerate for 30 minutes.

4. Preheat oven to 325°F. Line two cookie sheet pans with parchment paper.

5. On a lightly floured surface, roll out the dough to ¼-inch thickness. Cut out the cookies using a floured cookie cutter. Place the cookies on the prepared baking pans.

6. Bake 15 to 18 minutes. Let cool completely.

Assemble: Spread a tablespoon of the Nutella on the bottom side of half of the cookies. Top with the rest of the cookies.

Microwave the chocolate chips until melted, stirring occasionally. Drizzle the melted chocolate over the cookies. Let set for 15 minutes.

Add Some Love...

These chocolate shortbread cookies are friends with almost all the fillings: vanilla buttercream, dulce de leche, chocolate ganache, cream cheese frosting, peanut butter, you name it.

Gingerbread Gift Boxes

• Makes 3 big boxes and 3 small boxes •

A completely edible holiday gift inside and out—delicious gingerbread gift boxes filled with your choice of goodies. This holiday, let's ditch the idea of building a labor-intensive gingerbread house that either takes a village to consume or eventually goes to the trash after a little was eaten, but make these gingerbread boxes in a more thoughtful size.

Gingerbread Cookies

½ cup unsalted butter, softened

½ cup brown sugar

1 large egg, room temperature

½ cup molasses

3 cups flour

½ tsp. baking soda

½ tsp. salt

2 tsp. ground cinnamon

2 tsp. ground ginger

Royal Icing

2 large egg whites

2½ cups powdered sugar

1 tsp. lemon juice

Gingerbread Cookies

1. In the bowl of a standing mixer fitted with a paddle attachment, beat the butter and sugar on medium speed until light and fluffy, about 5 minutes.

2. Beat in the egg and molasses until combined.

3. Sift in the flour, baking soda, salt, and spices. Mix on low speed until just incorporated.

4. Gather and form a dough. Cover with plastic wrap and refrigerate for 30 minutes.

5. Preheat oven to 350°F. Line two cookie sheet pans with parchment paper

6. On a lightly floured surface, roll out the dough to ¼-inch thickness. Use a floured pizza cutter and a ruler to cut dough into eighteen 3-inch squares (for big boxes) and eighteen 2-inch squares (for small boxes). Shape six small dough balls for the lid handles. Place the cookies on the prepared baking pans.

7. Bake 12 to 15 minutes. Let cool completely

Royal Icing

1. In the bowl of a standing mixer fitted with a whisk, beat the egg whites on medium speed until foamy. Gradually add the sugar. Continue mixing until the icing is thickened and smooth.

2. Mix in the lemon juice until combined.

3. Transfer the icing to a piping bag with a small round tip.

Assemble: Pipe the royal icing along the edges of the cookie squares. Adhere the sides to create individual boxes.

Pipe more icing over to hide the edges.

Glue the cookie balls in the center of the cookie pieces with the royal icing to make the lids of the boxes.

Add Some Love...

Get kids involved! I know how messy and frustrating it can be to build a gigantic gingerbread house with kids, whenat the end what they all care about is eating the candy and you are left to finish that game alone! Let's scale down to building adorable gift boxes. More manageable for adults. More achievable for kids.

Roasted Strawberry Jam
Shortbread Sandwich Cookies

• Makes 20 sandwich cookies •

Pretty, delicious, and very addictive, these buttery shortbread cookies with sweet roasted strawberry jam are so easy to put together. The lovely ruby-red shown through the center makes these cookies a delectable gift during the holidays.

Roasted Strawberry Jam

2 cups fresh or frozen strawberries

¼ cup granulated sugar

1 Tbsp. balsamic vinegar

Shortbread Cookies

1 cup unsalted butter, softened

½ cup +1 Tbsp. powdered sugar

1 tsp. vanilla extract

2 cups flour

½ tsp. salt

Roasted Strawberry Jam

1. Preheat oven to 350°F.

2. In an 8-inch square baking pan, mix all the ingredients until the strawberries are well coated with sugar.

3. Spread the mixture in a single layer. Roast the strawberries for an hour. Stir once halfway through.

4. Mash the mixture with a fork. Let cool completely.

Shortbread Cookies

1. In the bowl of a standing mixer fitted with a paddle attachment, beat the butter and ½ cup of the powdered sugar on medium speed until light and fluffy, about 5 minutes.

2. Mix in the vanilla until combined.

3. Sift in the flour and salt. Mix on low speed until just incorporated.

4. Gather and form a dough. Cover with plastic wrap and refrigerate for 30 minutes.

5. Preheat oven to 325°F. Line two cookie sheet pans with parchment paper.

6. On a lightly floured surface, roll out the dough to ¼-inch thickness. Cut into stars using a floured cookie cutter. Cut out the center from half of the cookies using a smaller cookie cutter. Place the cookies on the prepared baking pans.

7. Bake 15 to 18 minutes. Let cool completely.

8. Spread a teaspoon of the strawberry jam on the bottom side of the remaining cookies.

9. Top with the center cut-out cookies.

10. Sprinkle the remaining powdered sugar over the cookies.

Add Some Love...

Try to add a layer of peanut butter with the strawberry jam, and you have a classic and nourishing peanut butter and jam sandwich in a cookie form!

Chewy Ginger Cookies with Lemon Cream Cheese Frosting

• Makes 18 sandwich cookies •

Fluffy lemon-flavored cream cheese frosting makes the perfect glue between two crisp and chewy ginger cookies. Warming spices with a luscious touch of citrus! If you are not a fan of sandwich cookies, simply opt out of the frosting. The cookies themselves are pure perfection on their own. A unique take on the traditional cut-out men.

Chewy Ginger Cookies

¾ cup unsalted butter, softened
1 cup granulated sugar
1 large egg, room temperature
¼ cup molasses
2 cups flour
2 tsp. baking soda
½ tsp. salt
½ tsp. ground cinnamon
½ tsp. ground ginger
¼ tsp. allspice

Lemon Cream Cheese Frosting

½ cup cream cheese, softened
¼ cup unsalted butter, softened
½ Tbsp. lemon juice
½ cup powdered sugar

Chewy Ginger Cookie

1. Preheat oven to 325°F. Line two cookie sheet pans with parchment paper.

2. In the bowl of a standing mixer fitted with a paddle attachment, beat the butter and sugar on medium speed until light and fluffy, about 5 minutes.

3. Beat in the egg and molasses until combined.

4. Sift in the flour, baking soda, salt, and spices. Mix on low speed until just incorporated.

5. Shape the dough into tablespoon-sized balls.

6. Place on the prepared baking pans. Leave two inches between cookies.

7. Bake 12 to 15 minutes. Let cool completely.

Lemon Cream Cheese Frosting

1. In the bowl of a standing mixer fitted with a paddle attachment, beat the cream cheese, butter, and lemon juice on medium speed for 2 minutes.

2. Add the powdered sugar and continue beating on low speed until incorporated. Turn up the speed to medium, and beat the frosting until light and fluffy, about 5 minutes.

3. Transfer the frosting to a piping bag with a round tip.

4. Assemble: Pipe the frosting on the bottom side of half of the cookies. Top with the rest of the cookies.

Add Some Love...

Like my daughter always said, the best sandwich cookie is an ice cream sandwich cookie! And the perfect texture of these ginger cookies is meant to go with ice cream. Tender and moist even when frozen, they don't need to be limited to a Christmas cookie; in fact, they are fantastic in the summertime!

Salted Chocolate Ganache Macarons

• Makes 30 sandwich cookies •

Don't let the word macarons scare you away! If made correctly, these light and delicious treats will add a classy French flair to any of your cookie dishes. However, sometimes I do find macarons a little too sweet for my taste. To balance that sweetness, I like to add a little salt in the filling. The salted chocolate ganache intensifies the overall macaron flavor, but also beautifully plays off the sweetness.

Macaron Shells

1 cup powdered sugar
1 Tbsp. cocoa powder
¾ cup almond flour
2 large egg whites
¼ cup granulated sugar
1 tsp. vanilla extract

Chocolate Ganache

100 grams dark chocolate, cut into
    small pieces
1/3 cup heavy whipping cream
½ tsp. sea salt

Macaron Shells

1. Line two cookie sheet pans with parchment paper.

2. In a food processor, blend the powdered sugar, cocoa powder, and almond flour until finely ground. Sift the mixture into a large bowl.

3. In the bowl of a standing mixer fitted with a whisk, beat the egg whites on medium speed until foamy. Reduce the speed to low and gradually add the granulated sugar, a tablespoon at a time.

4. Add the vanilla. Increase the speed to high and beat until firm peaks form, about 5 minutes.

5. Pour the almond flour mixture over the egg whites. Use a spatula to gently fold the almond flour mixture into the egg whites until the ingredients are combined and the mixture has loosened and falls in a ribbon from the spatula.

6. Transfer the mixture to a piping bag with a round tip. Pipe 1½-inch circles onto the parchment paper.

7. Tap the bottom of each sheet on the work surface to release trapped air bubbles.

8. Let the cookies sit for at least 30 minutes to develop their crusts.

9. Preheat oven to 325°F. Bake the macarons 10 to 12 minutes, until set but not browned. Let cool completely.

10. Gently peel half of the cookies from the parchment paper and turn them upside down.

Chocolate Ganache

1. Microwave the cream on high for 45 seconds. Pour the hot cream over the chocolate. Let sit for a minute. Add the sea salt, then whisk together until smooth. Let cool completely.

Assemble: Spoon the ganache on each of the upside-down macaron shells. Place the top shell on top. Gently press down a little.

Add Some Love...

Macarons are notoriously temperamental. My first time making macarons was a massive failure, the second time was slightly better, and the third time was quite a success, although they were not perfect in appearance. I gifted that batch to one of my best friends, who is a huge macaron fan with a note, "My third attempt so far . . . will keep working on it. Hope you enjoy them!" Her response without even opening the box, "I knew they would be the best I've ever had because of that crazy amount of love you put in there!"

Spiced Chocolate Almond Icebox Cookies

• Makes 40 cookies •

These delicious little cut-and-bake morsels are wonderfully flavored with ground cinnamon, ginger, and allspice. Chocolate chunks and finely ground almonds create the extra crunch and nutty flavor you didn't even know you needed.

½ cup unsalted butter, softened
½ cup granulated sugar
1 large egg, room temperature
1½ cups flour
1 tsp. salt
½ tsp. ground cinnamon

½ tsp. ground ginger
½ tsp. ground allspice
½ cup whole almonds
½ cup dark chocolate chunks, finely chopped

Spiced Chocolate Almond Icebox Cookies

1. In the bowl of a standing mixer fitted with a paddle attachment, beat the butter and sugar on medium speed until light and fluffy, about 5 minutes.

2. Mix in the egg until combined.

3. Sift in the flour, salt, and spices. Mix on low speed until just incorporated.

4. Add in the almonds and chocolate until combined.

5. Gather and form a 10-inch log. Cover with plastic wrap and refrigerate the dough until very firm, at least 2 hours.

6. Preheat oven to 350°F. Line two cookie sheet pans with parchment paper.

7. Cut the dough crosswise into ¼-inch thick slices.

8. Bake the cookies for 12 to 15 minutes.

9. Let cool completely.

Add Some Love...

Form the cookie dough in a long rectangular, triangular, or square-shaped log to create your preferred shape.

Vanilla and Raspberry Marbled Macarons

• Makes 30 sandwich cookies •

Macarons can be made with almost any flavor combinations you can think of.
These ones are filled with sweet vanilla buttercream and fruity raspberry jam and decorated
with festive marbled royal icing. A stunningly beautiful finale to your holiday dinner.

Macaron Shells

1 cup powdered sugar
¾ cup almond flour
2 large egg whites
¼ cup granulated sugar
1 tsp. vanilla extract

Royal Icing

1 large egg white

1 cup powdered sugar
1 tsp. lemon juice
1–2 drops red food coloring paste

Vanilla Raspberry Filling

½ cup unsalted butter, softened
1 cup powdered sugar
1 tsp. vanilla extract
½ cup raspberry jam

Macaron Shells

1. Line two cookie sheet pans with parchment paper.

2. In a food processor, blend the powdered sugar and almond flour until finely ground. Sift the mixture into a large bowl.

3. In the bowl of a standing mixer fitted with a whisk, beat the egg whites on medium speed until foamy. Reduce the speed to low, and gradually add the granulated sugar, a tablespoon at a time.

4. Add the vanilla. Increase the speed to high and beat until firm peaks form, about 5 minutes.

5. Pour the almond flour mixture over the egg whites. Using a spatula, gently fold the almond flour mixture into the egg whites until the ingredients are combined and the mixture has loosened and falls in a ribbon from the spatula.

6. Transfer the mixture to a piping bag with a round tip. Pipe 1½-inch circles onto the parchment paper.

7. Tap the bottom of each sheet on the work surface to release trapped air bubbles.

8. Let the cookies sit for at least 30 minutes to develop their crusts.

9. Preheat oven to 325°F. Bake the macarons for 10 to 12 minutes, until set but not browned. Let cool completely.

10. Gently peel half of the cookies from the parchment paper and turn them upside down.

Vanilla and Raspberry Marbled Macarons
(continued)

Royal Icing

1. In the bowl of a standing mixer fitted with a whisk, beat the egg white on medium speed until foamy. Gradually add the powdered sugar. Continue mixing until the icing is thickened and smooth.

2. Mix in the lemon juice until combined.

3. Pour half of the icing into a small bowl. Add a drop of food coloring. Gently swirl with a toothpick. Carefully dip the tops of half of the macaron shells into the icing, and allow any excess to drip off. Let the icing dry completely, at least 4 hours.

Vanilla Raspberry Filling

1. In the bowl of a standing mixer fitted with a paddle attachment, beat the butter on medium speed for 2 minutes. Add the powdered sugar and vanilla and continue beating on low speed until incorporated. Turn up the speed to medium, and beat the buttercream until light and fluffy, about 5 minutes.

2. Transfer the buttercream to a piping bag with a small round tip.

Assemble: Pipe the buttercream along the edge of each bottom macaron shell. Fill in a teaspoon of raspberry jam. Place the top shell on top. Gently press down a little.

Add Some Love...

The marbled royal icing is so fun, beautiful, and surprisingly easy to work with to decorate your macarons or other cookies. Try using two or more colors to create a whimsical marble effect. You could also use chocolate or white chocolate for your dip if you prefer.

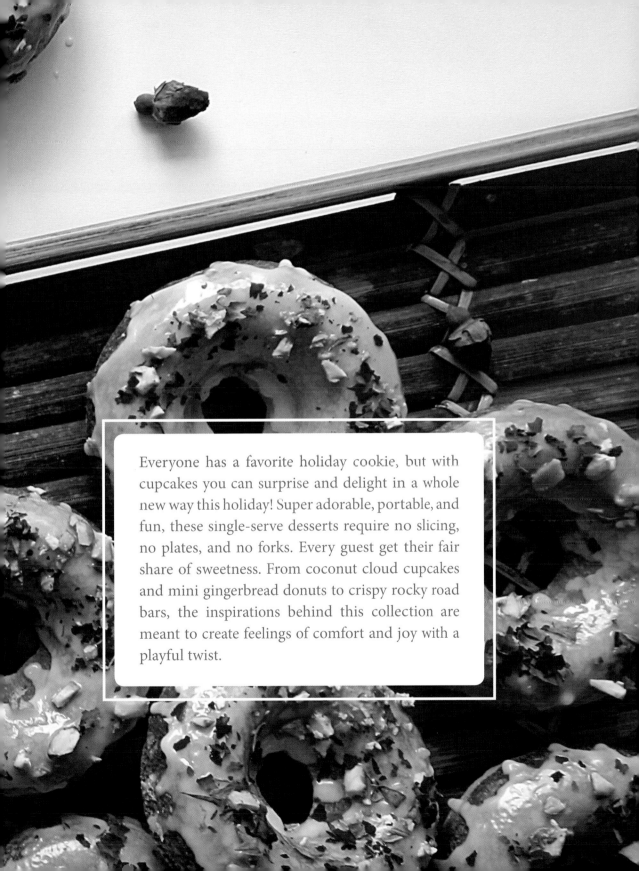

Everyone has a favorite holiday cookie, but with cupcakes you can surprise and delight in a whole new way this holiday! Super adorable, portable, and fun, these single-serve desserts require no slicing, no plates, and no forks. Every guest get their fair share of sweetness. From coconut cloud cupcakes and mini gingerbread donuts to crispy rocky road bars, the inspirations behind this collection are meant to create feelings of comfort and joy with a playful twist.

Cupcakes | Donuts | Bars

Coconut Cloud Cupcakes

• Makes 15 cupcakes •

*Light, airy angel food cake scented with coconut and topped with coconut whipped cream,
these adorable treats in petite cupcake presentation make you feel like you are nibbling clouds.
Since angel food cake is naturally fat-free, it's okay if you go for a second or third one.*

Coconut Angel Food Cupcakes

½ cup cake flour

¾ cup powdered sugar

½ tsp. salt

6 large egg whites

½ tsp. cream of tartar

1 tsp. coconut extract

¼ cup granulated sugar

Coconut Whipped Cream

1 cup coconut cream

1 cup heavy whipping cream

¼ cup powdered sugar

Toppings

½ cup sweetened coconut flakes

Coconut Angel Food Cupcakes

1. Preheat oven to 350°F. Line two muffin tins with liners.

2. In a large bowl, sift the flour, powdered sugar, and salt.

3. In the bowl of a standing mixer fitted with a whisk, beat the egg whites, cream of tartar, and coconut extract on medium speed until foamy.

4. Reduce the speed to low and gradually add the sugar, a tablespoon at a time.

5. Increase the speed to high and beat until firm peaks from, about 5 minutes.

6. Gently fold the flour mixture into the egg white mixture until just incorporated.

7. Evenly divide the batter among the prepared muffin cups, filling them two-thirds full.

8. Bake 15 to 20 minutes, until a toothpick inserted in the cupcake center comes out clean.

9. Let cool completely.

Coconut Whipped Cream

1. In the bowl of a standing mixer fitted with a whisk, beat the creams and sugar on low speed until soft peaks form. Continue beating on medium speed until firm peaks form.

2. Transfer the whipped cream to a piping bag with a round tip.

Assemble: Pipe the whipped cream on the cooled cupcakes. Sprinkle coconut flakes on top.

Add Some Love...

Can't find canned coconut cream? No worries! All you have to do is to refrigerate a can of coconut milk overnight. The next day, open the can and scoop out the top layer of white and fatty goodness. That's coconut cream! Save the coconut water for smoothies.

Tahini Chocolate Banana Cupcakes

• Makes 12 cupcakes •

Tahini? In a cupcake? Yep! That condiment you put in your hummus is about to get a serious upgrade. Its slightly nutty flavor and silky-smooth texture make for the perfect addition to these cupcakes. Switch things up a bit from your basic peanut butter buttercream, and make this tahini version.

Banana Cupcakes

1¾ cups flour
1 tsp. baking powder
1 tsp. baking soda
½ tsp. salt
3 large eggs, room temperature
¾ cup granulated sugar
2 large overripe bananas, mashed
¾ cup vegetable oil
50 grams dark chocolate, melted
½ cup sesame seeds, lightly toasted

Tahini Buttercream

1 cup unsalted butter, softened
½ cup tahini
2 cups powdered sugar

Toppings

¼ cup chocolate shavings
12 banana slices

Banana Cupcakes

1. Preheat oven to 350°F. Line a muffin tin with liners.

2. In a large bowl, whisk together the flour, baking powder, baking soda, and salt.

3. In another large bowl, whisk together the eggs, sugar, bananas, and oil until combined.

4. Stir in the flour mixture until just incorporated.

5. Evenly divide the batter among the prepared muffin cups, filling them two-thirds full.

6. Bake 15 to 20 minutes. Let cool completely.

7. Dip each cupcake in the melted chocolate upside down to coat the top, and allow any excess to drip off.

8. Sprinkle the sesame seeds on top.

9. Let the chocolate set, about 10 minutes.

Tahini Buttercream

1. In the bowl of a standing mixer with a paddle attachment, beat the butter and tahini on medium speed for 2 minutes.

2. Add the powdered sugar and continue beating on low speed until incorporated. Turn up the speed to medium, and beat the buttercream until light and fluffy, about 5 minutes.

3. Frost the cupcakes with the buttercream.

4. Garnish with chocolate shavings and banana slices.

Add Some Love...

Do not throw away those overripe dark bananas! They are your secret ingredients for the best banana cake. The blacker, the better! They will deliver the most banana flavor possible, and ensure a very banana-y treat. Their natural sweetness helps to cut off the amount of additional granulated sugar. Start freezing your ripe bananas.

Crispy Rocky Road Bars

• Makes 16 bars •

Crispy, chocolatey, gooey, no-bake, versatile, fun, kid-friendly, adult-friendly . . .
I mean, do I need to say more? Cheers to the kid that lives in all of us!

---

200 grams dark chocolate, cut into chunks
1 cup peanut butter

5 cups crisp rice cereal
3 cup marshmallows, frozen

Crispy Rocky Road Bars

1. Line an 8-inch square baking pan with parchment paper.

2. Microwave the chocolate and peanut butter on high for a minute. Stir and microwave more, in 10-second intervals, until the mixture is completely melted and smooth.

3. Let cool slightly.

4. Mix in the cereal and marshmallows.

5. Pour the mixture into the prepared pan. Press it down firmly, and level the top.

6. Refrigerate until set, about 30 minutes.

7. Cut into squares with a sharp knife.

Add Some Love...

This recipe takes no time to put together! Why not spend another 10 minutes to freeze your marshmallows, so they will stay nice and whole in the warm chocolate mixture, instead of melting and disappearing all over!

Easy-Peasy Winning Chocolate Cupcakes

• Makes 12 cupcakes •

Versatile, delicious, and incredibly simple, this one-bowl chocolate cupcake recipe has never failed to win me compliments. I always come to my go-to recipe when I need to whip up something really quick but amazing for a party or potluck gathering. These chocolate cupcakes hold a special place in my baking heart. Seriously, there is no reason to find a better version.

Chocolate Cupcakes

1 cup flour
¼ cup cocoa powder, sifted
1 cup granulated sugar
1 tsp. baking powder
1 tsp. baking soda
½ tsp. salt
1 large egg, room temperature
½ cup plain yogurt, room temperature
¼ cup vegetable oil
1 Tbsp. vanilla extract
½ cup hot water

Chocolate Glaze

100 grams dark chocolate, cut into small pieces
1/3 cup heavy whipping cream
1 Tbsp. unsalted butter

Chocolate Cupcakes

1. Preheat oven to 350°F. Line a muffin tin with liners.

2. Whisk together the flour, cocoa powder, sugar, baking powder, baking soda, and salt.

3. Stir in the egg, yogurt, oil, and vanilla until combined.

4. Mix in the hot water slowly until the mixture becomes smooth.

5. Evenly divide the batter among the prepared muffin cups, filling them two-thirds full.

6. Bake 15 to 20 minutes. Let cool completely.

Chocolate Glaze

1. Microwave the cream on high for 45 seconds. Pour the hot cream over the chocolate and butter. Let sit for a minute, then whisk together until smooth.

2. Dip each cupcake in the glaze upside down to coat the top, and allow any excess to drip off.

3. Let the glaze set, about 10 minutes.

Add Some Love...

You can decorate the cupcakes with chocolate buttercream, cream cheese frosting, whipped cream with berries, or just a dusting of powdered sugar.

Mini Gingerbread Donuts

• Makes 24 mini donuts •

As much as these spice-filled donuts will make your house smell like Christmas, they will also give you the familiar old-fashioned donut taste without all the hassle of rolling, cutting, and frying the dough. Great breakfast treat or delicious snack any time of the day!

Gingerbread Donuts

1¼ cups flour
1 tsp. baking powder
½ tsp. baking soda
½ tsp. salt
½ tsp. ground cinnamon
½ tsp. ground ginger
½ tsp. allspice
1/3 cup unsalted butter, melted and cooled
½ cup granulated sugar
1 large egg, room temperature
2 Tbsp. molasses
1 tsp. vanilla extract
½ cup buttermilk, room temperature

Cinnamon Sugar

¼ cup granulated sugar
1 tsp. ground cinnamon

Donuts

1. Preheat oven to 350°F. Grease two mini donut pans.

2. In a large bowl, whisk together the flour, baking powder, baking soda, salt, and spices.

3. In another large bowl, whisk together the melted butter, sugar, egg, and molasses.

4. Mix in half of the flour mixture, buttermilk, and the remaining flour mixture. Mix until just incorporated between each addition.

5. Transfer the batter to a piping bag with a round tip. Pipe the batter in the prepared pan, filling it two-thirds full.

6. Bake for 8 to 10 minutes. Let cool slightly.

Cinnamon Sugar

1. Mix together all the ingredients.

Assemble: Coat the warm donuts with the cinnamon sugar.

Add Some Love...

To "glaze" someone over, you can easily make a bowl of glaze by mixing a cup of powdered sugar with ¼ cup milk, orange juice, or lemon juice. Add your favorite flavor (vanilla or almond extract), or a few drops of food coloring paste.

Macadamia and Dried Cranberry Blondies

• Makes 16 blondies •

Literally possessing all the flavors and textures you can name, these blondies are sweet, nutty, tart, gooey, tender, crunchy. . . . All decadent and very addictive!

1½ cups flour
1 tsp. baking powder
½ tsp. salt
1¼ cups unsalted butter, melted and cooled
1½ cups brown sugar

2 large eggs, room temperature
1 tsp. vanilla extract
1 cup macadamia nuts
1 cup dried cranberries
¼ cup white chocolate chips

Macadamia and Dried Cranberry Blondies

1. Preheat oven to 350°F. Grease and line an 8-inch square baking pan with parchment paper.

2. In a large bowl, whisk together the flour, baking powder, and salt.

3. In another large bowl, whisk together the melted butter and brown sugar until combined. Whisk in the eggs and vanilla until combined.

4. Fold in the flour mixture, nuts, and dried cranberries until just incorporated.

5. Pour the batter into the prepared pan.

6. Bake 20 to 25 minutes, until the top is golden brown.

7. Let cool completely. Cut into squares with a sharp knife.

8. Microwave the white chocolate chips until melted, stirring occasionally. Drizzle the melted chocolate over the blondies. Let set for 15 minutes.

Add Some Love...

As lovely as these blondies are nicely-packed as gift, they are also wonderful as dessert after dinner. Warm them up a little in the oven, and serve them with vanilla ice cream.

Red Velvet Cupcakes

• Makes 12 cupcakes •

The foolproof recipe that I always come back to, these red velvet cupcakes can easily be called the best. They are as photogenic as they are delicious—gorgeous red, moist, fluffy, with a hint of chocolate, and topped with a luscious cream cheese frosting. Just like what you get from high-end bakeries.

Red Velvet Cupcakes

1½ cups flour

1 tsp. baking powder

1 tsp. baking soda

½ tsp. salt

1½ Tbsp. cocoa powder

¾ cup canola oil

1 cup granulated sugar

1 large egg, room temperature

1 cup buttermilk, room temperature

1 tsp. vanilla extract

1 Tbsp. red food coloring paste

Vanilla Cream Cheese Frosting

1 cup cream cheese, softened

½ cup unsalted butter, softened

1 Tbsp. vanilla extract

2 cups powdered sugar

Red Velvet Cupcakes

1. Preheat oven to 350°F. Line a muffin tin with liners.

2. In a large bowl, whisk together the flour, baking powder, baking soda, salt, and cocoa powder.

3. In another large bowl, whisk together the oil, sugar, egg, buttermilk, vanilla, and food coloring.

4. Mix in the flour mixture until just incorporated.

5. Evenly divide the batter among the prepared muffin cups, filling them two-thirds full.

6. Bake 15 to 20 minutes. Let cool completely.

Vanilla Cream Cheese Frosting

1. In the bowl of a standing mixer fitted with a paddle attachment, beat the cream cheese, butter, and vanilla on medium speed for 2 minutes.

2. Add the powdered sugar and continue beating on low speed until incorporated. Turn up the speed to medium, and beat the frosting until light and fluffy, about 5 minutes.

Assemble: Frost the cupcakes with the frosting.

Add Some Love...

Buttermilk is a key element to this recipe. The acidic liquid is needed to combine with the baking soda to get the perfect texture. You can make your own buttermilk if you don't have any! Just mix a cup of milk with a tablespoon of lemon juice. Stir together and let sit for 5 minutes. You are all set!

Cardamom and Pistachio Donuts

• Makes 12 donuts •

Spice up your regular donuts with tons of interesting flavor—aromatic cardamom, nutty pistachios, and a bright note of lemon. Also, these baked donuts are a healthier alternative to fried donuts.

Cardamom Donuts

1¼ cups flour
1 tsp. baking powder
½ tsp. baking soda
½ tsp. salt
1 tsp. cardamom
1/3 cup unsalted butter, melted and cooled
½ cup granulated sugar
1 large egg, room temperature

1 tsp. vanilla extract
½ cup buttermilk, room temperature

Lemon Glaze

1 cup powdered sugar
¼ cup lemon juice

Toppings

¼ cup chopped pistachios
1 Tbsp. dried rose petals

Donuts

1. Preheat oven to 350°F. Grease two donut pans.

2. In a large bowl, sift together the flour, baking powder, baking soda, salt, and cardamom

3. In another large bowl, whisk together the melted butter, sugar, egg, and vanilla.

4. Mix in half of the flour mixture, buttermilk, and the remaining flour mixture. Mix until just incorporated between each addition.

5. Transfer the batter to a piping bag with a round tip. Pipe the batter into the prepared pans, filling them two-thirds full.

6. Bake 15 to 20 minutes. Let cool slightly.

Lemon Glaze

1. Mix together all the ingredients.

Assemble: Dip the top of each donut into the glaze, and allow any excess to drip off.

Top with the pistachios and rose petals.

Let the glaze set for 30 minutes before serving.

Add Some Love...

Use fresh rose petals to decorate your donuts if you prefer. They are completely edible.

Mini Hazelnut and Toasted Marshmallow Cream Puffs

• Makes 30 cream puffs •

You don't have to be an expert pastry chef to create delicate cream puffs at home. All you need is a few basic ingredients. By following some simple steps, you will be amazed by how easy it is to create these light and airy confections. Filled with hazelnut-infused pastry cream and toasted marshmallow frosting, these petite treats are too pretty to eat, but also too delicious not to.

Hazelnut Pastry Cream

2 cups milk
1 cup hazelnuts, lightly toasted
3 egg yolks
1/3 cup granulated sugar
¼ cup cornstarch

Cream Puff Shells

1 cup water
½ cup unsalted butter
½ tsp. salt
1 cup flour
4 large eggs

Toasted Marshmallow Frosting

½ cup granulated sugar
2 egg whites
½ tsp. vanilla extract

Hazelnut Pastry Cream

1. In a saucepan, cook the milk and hazelnuts over medium heat to bring the mixture just to a boil. Stir occasionally.

2. Remove from heat. Let the hazelnuts infuse the milk for 30 minutes. Stir occasionally.

3. Strain the hazelnuts away from the milk. Keep the milk.

4. In a small bowl, whisk together the egg yolks and sugar until the mixture becomes light and fluffy.

5. Whisk in the cornstarch until smooth.

6. Slowly whisk one third of the milk mixture into the egg mixture. Pour the milk-egg mixture back to the saucepan. Cook on low heat and whisk continuously until the custard is thickened, about 3 minutes.

7. Strain the custard to make it smooth.

8. Let cool to room temperature.

9. Place a plastic wrap directly on the surface of the pastry cream. Refrigerate for at least 2 hours to set.

Mini Hazelnut and Toasted Marshmallow Cream Puffs
(continued)

Cream Puff Shells

1. Preheat oven to 400°F. Line two cookie sheet pans with parchment paper.

2. Cook the water, butter, and salt on medium heat to bring the mixture just to a boil.

3. Stir in the flour vigorously until the mixture begins to pull away from the sides of the pan and comes together in a ball, about 2 minutes.

4. Remove from heat. Let cool for 10 minutes.

5. Transfer the dough to a food processor. Beat in the eggs, one at a time. Blend until incorporated between each addition.

6. Spoon 30 dough balls onto the prepared pans. Smooth the tops with a wet finger.

7. Bake 15 to 20 minutes, until the tops are golden brown.

8. Let cool completely.

Toasted Marshmallow Frosting

1. Set the bowl of a standing mixer over a pan of simmering water. Whisk the sugar and egg whites until the sugar is dissolved and the egg whites are warm to touch.

2. Transfer the bowl to the standing mixer fitted with a whisk and beat on high speed until the frosting forms firm peaks.

3. Mix in the vanilla until combined.

4. Transfer the frosting to a piping bag with a round tip.

Assemble: Cut off the top of each cream puff shell. Fill with a tablespoon of the hazelnut pastry cream. Pipe the meringue frosting on top. Top with the cream puff top shell. Pipe a little more meringue frosting on the cream puff. Sprinkle with the toasted hazelnut. Use a kitchen torch to lightly brown the frosting.

Add Some Love...

Let's have a cream puff party! Get your dessert table ready with whipped cream, fresh berries, ice cream, chocolate sauce, salted caramel, and so on. Bake up a batch of cream puff shells, and let your guests go crazy and creative with the fillings.

Let's be honest, doesn't store-bought chocolate sound a little like a "I hope you will like it" kind of gift? And you know, making one-of-a-kind chocolate for your chocoholic friends is just an ice-cube tray away! It's fun, it's easy, and the receiver will think you went through a lot of trouble and be pleasantly surprised! Just as delicious and festive, cake pops are the whimsical partner to other petite treats on the dessert table. Also, they make delightful novelty food gifts.

Confections

Holiday Chocolate Rounds

• Makes 12 chocolate rounds •

Intricate, elegant, and delicious, each of the chocolate rounds are a unique combination of flavors and textures. They are delightfully easy to make, but the end results are so delicate and beautiful that you'd be forgiven for thinking you'd bought them from an luxurious chocolatier.

Toppings

Assorted nuts/seeds (walnuts, pecans, almonds, cashews, hazelnuts, pistachios, pumpkin seeds, sunflower seeds)

Assorted dried fruits (cranberries, raspberries, blueberries, strawberries, cherries, apricots, raisins, candied ginger, orange rind, lemon rind)

Assorted dried herbs (lavender, rose petals, sage, rosemary)

Others (sea salt flakes, coconut flakes, sprinkles)

Chocolate Base

200 grams good-quality dark chocolate

Toppings

1. Preheat oven to 350°F. Line a cookie sheet pan with parchment paper. Toast the nuts or seeds for 5 to 10 minutes. Let cool completely.

2. Roughly chop the larger nuts or dried fruits into smaller pieces.

Add Some Love...

Use the best chocolate you can get, because it's the star of the show. And for the toppings, only the sky is the limit! Just think up some flavor combos that will knock the socks off of whoever you are giving the chocolate to. I'm thinking chilli flakes . . .

Chocolate Base

1. Set a bowl over a pan of simmering water. Melt the chocolate while stirring occasionally.

2. Spoon the melted chocolate in a silicon ice cube tray, chocolate mold, or mini cupcake pan. Tap the tray gently on the counter to remove the air bubbles in the chocolate.

3. Place two or three toppings on the chocolate. Use your finger to gently press the toppings into the chocolate to make sure they stick.

4. Place the chocolate in the refrigerator for 30 minutes to set.

5. Remove the chocolate carefully from the tray.

Celebration Cake Pops

• Makes 45 cake pops •

There is no better time than a happy occasion to indulge yourself into some special treats, whether it's a birthday, baby shower, wedding, or as simple as your kid's playdate. Like a party for your palate, cake pops are a sweet mix of cake and icing inside and a fun chocolate coating with sprinkles on the outside. A whimsical treat to eat and look at!

Vanilla Cake

1 ¼ cups flour
1 tsp. baking powder
1 tsp. baking soda
½ tsp. salt
½ cup unsalted butter, softened
1 cup granulated sugar
2 large eggs
1 tsp. vanilla extract
1 cup milk, room temperature

Vanilla Buttercream

½ cup unsalted butter, softened
1 cup powdered sugar
½ tsp. vanilla extract

Chocolate Coating

300 grams chocolate or candy coating
1 Tbsp. vegetable oil
Sprinkles of your choice

Vanilla Cake

1. Preheat oven to 350°F. Grease and line an 8-inch cake pan with parchment paper.

2. Whisk together the flour, baking powder, baking soda, and salt.

3. In the bowl of a standing mixer fitted with a paddle attachment, beat the butter and sugar on medium speed until light and fluffy, about 5 minutes.

4. Beat in the eggs, one at a time, followed by the vanilla.

5. With the mixer on low, mix in half of the flour mixture, the milk, and the remaining half of the flour mixture. Mix until just incorporated between each addition.

6. Pour the batter into the prepared pan. Bake 20 to 25 minutes, until a toothpick inserted in the cake center comes out clean.

7. Let the cake cool in the pan for 10 minutes. Remove from the pan, and let cool completely.

Vanilla Buttercream

1. In a bowl of a standing mixer with a paddle attachment, beat the butter on medium speed for 2 minutes.

2. Add the sugar and vanilla and continue beating on low speed until incorporated. Turn up the speed to medium, and beat the buttercream until light and fluffy, about 5 minutes.

Assemble: Line two cookie sheet pans with parchment paper.

Break the cooled cake into a few big pieces by hand.

Place them into the bowl of a standing mixer fitted with a paddle attachment. Mix on medium speed until the cake turns into crumbs.

Mix in a cup of buttercream until the mixture becomes a dough. Add more buttercream if needed.

Form the dough into tablespoon-sized balls. Place them on the prepared pans. Refrigerate for 30 minutes.

Microwave the chocolate on high for a minute. Stir and microwave more, in 10-second intervals, until the chocolate is completely melted and smooth.

Add the tablespoon of oil, if needed, to thin the melted chocolate.

Dip one end of a lollipop stick a half inch into the chocolate. Insert into the center of the cake ball. Repeat with the rest of the cake balls.

Dip each cake ball in the chocolate. Gently tap off excess. Place onto parchment paper. Decorate with sprinkles immediately, and let dry completely. Repeat with the remaining cake pops.

Add Some Love...

You can go with your favorite cake and frosting recipes to create your own flavor. When it comes to the perfect cake and frosting portion, it's important to add the frosting to the cake crumbs gradually, and mix until it just forms dough consistency: not so wet that it tastes like grease, and not so dry that the cake ball falls apart.

Snowballs

• Makes 30 balls •

*If you can spare 10 minutes in your life, make these buttery and nutty cookie balls
to cheer up your loved ones! They are literally the easiest treat to make.
I seriously doubt that anyone would not become addicted to these.*

---

1 cup cake flour
1½ cups nuts of your choice (walnuts,
    pecans, almonds, cashews, hazelnuts or
    pistachios)
1 tsp. salt

2 Tbsp. granulated sugar
1 tsp. vanilla extract
½ cup unsalted butter, softened
1 cup powdered sugar

Snowballs

1. Preheat oven to 300°F. Line two cookie sheet pans with parchment paper.

2. In a food processor, blend together the flour, nuts, salt, and sugar, until the nuts are finely chopped.

3. Mix in vanilla until combined.

4. Scatter in the butter in small pieces. Mix until the mixture resembles wet sand.

5. Shape the dough into tablespoon-sized balls. Place them on the prepared pans, leaving an inch apart between the balls.

6. Bake 30 to 35 minutes. Let cool for 10 minutes.

7. Roll them in the powdered sugar while they are still warm.

8. Let cool completely.

Add Some Love...

Thirty cookies may only be able to make two or three of your friends happy. Feel free to double or even triple this recipe to make more cookies!

Almond Praline Chocolates

• Makes 12 chocolates •

*Pay attention here, my friends! These chocolates are not your typical almond chocolates!
They are far beyond those. Inside the dark chocolate shell is a toasty, nutty, and subtly sweet
soft bite of caramelized almond paste. Forget about that box of "hope-you-like-it" chocolate, and
give your loved ones homemade, melt-in-your-mouth almond praline chocolates.*

¾ cup granulated sugar
2 Tbsp. water

1½ cups toasted whole almonds
200 grams good-quality dark chocolate

Almond Praline Chocolates

1. Cook the sugar and water over low heat until the mixture reaches a golden caramel color.

2. Remove from heat. Stir in the almonds to coat with the caramel.

3. Spread the mixture on a cookie sheet pan lined with parchment paper. Let cool for an hour.

4. Break the caramelized almonds into pieces.

5. In a food processor, blend the almonds into a paste.

6. Transfer the paste to a piping bag with a small tip.

7. Set a bowl over a pan of simmering water. Melt the chocolate while stirring occasionally.

8. Pour the chocolate into a silicone ice cube tray, chocolate mold, or mini cupcake pan. Let it sit for 10 seconds. Invert the mold to allow the excess to drip off.

9. Turn the mold back over. Use a metal scraper to clean off the chocolate excess on the sides.

10. Refrigerate the chocolate for 5 minutes.

11. Pipe 2 teaspoons of almond praline into the chocolate shells, leaving a thin gap between the praline surface and the top of the mold.

12. Pour the chocolate over the praline. Scrape the top clean to create a seal.

13. Refrigerate the chocolate for 5 minutes.

14. Release the chocolates from the mold. Decorate with the gold leaves.

Add Some Love...

If you are thinking about hazelnuts, pistachios, cashews, pecans, pine nuts . . . you are on the right track to go creative and beyond. This praline recipe goes well with almost all kinds of nuts. Try a mix of them!

Metric Conversion Chart

Volume		Weight		Temperature	
U.S.	**Metric**	**U.S.**	**Metric**	**°F**	**°C**
1 tsp.	5 ml	½ ounce	15 g	250	120
1 Tbsp.	15 ml	1 ounce	30 g	300	150
¼ cup	60 ml	3 ounces	90 g	325	160
⅓ cup	75 ml	4 ounces	115 g	350	180
½ cup	125 ml	8 ounces	225 g	375	190
⅔ cup	150 ml	12 ounces	350 g	400	200
¾ cup	175 ml	1 pound	450 g	425	220
1 cup	250 ml	2¼ pound	1 kg	450	230

Hugs and Kisses! Thank you!

It's natural to think that a book is made by the one person named on the cover, but the truth is far from it. I could not have ever done it without so many amazing people in my life, and I want to thank everyone who helped make my first cookbook a reality.

Thank you, Mommy, for teaching me the value of hard work. You are the only person who understands why I have to spend longer that it should take to decorate a cake.

To my mother-in-law and father-in-law—you are my second parents! Thank you for cooking us food, babysitting the kids, and always saying yes whenever I need help.

To my editor, Tracy—you made my dream come true! Thank you for seeing the potential in my work, offering me this opportunity, and helping this first-time author navigate through the whole publication process.

To my editor, Briana - thank you for jumping in and joining me on this journey! You are always there when I need help and advice!

To my designer, Shawnda—thank you for your patience and understanding. You turned my words and photographs into something beautiful, something that truly represents my style.

To the team at Cedar Fort—thank you for your expertise for bringing this book to life.

To Sandy and AK—you girls rock! Thank you for being silly with me all along. I know we will be teasing and crying together until the end of time.

To Eliza, Josephine, and Desiree—thank you for believing in me, supporting me, and being amazing friends over the years.

Thank you to all my friends and family who have shaped my journey and shared my stories along the road. I am so grateful to have you all in my life.

To my friends at farmer's markets—thank you for hanging with me every weekend. My weekends have become more fruitful and memorable.

To all of my many tasters—thank you for being adventurous enough to try my desserts. Your invaluable comments were hugely appreciated. You made my book better.

To my wonderful clients—thank you for your continuous support. *Oh Sweet Day!* would not be as sweet without your support.

To my blog and social media followers—thank you for your incredible support. This journey could not have happened without your every like and comment.

To Ethan and Maya—you are my lovely souls. Thank you for always being the first to raise your cups and say "Cheers!" at every dinner. Thank you for being so excited about this book. You are the reason why I do what I do. I hope I will make you proud.

To Matt—you are the light of my life. I wouldn't be me without you. Being a stubborn perfectionist, I thank you for listening to me, reasoning with me, doing many last-minute grocery runs, fixing my computer, making sure Netflix is working, eating my desserts, and making me laugh.

Index

T

V

W

Notes

About the Author

FANNY LAM is a self-taught baker and photographer. Her "less is more" approach goes hand-in-hand with her natural heartfelt enthusiasm for capturing the essence of her food. She makes friendly and comforting desserts look brand new and surprising.

She established herself as a successful blogger, social influencer, and online baker with the creation of her blog, *Oh Sweet Day!*. Her recipes have been featured on Huffington Post, Food52, The Kitchn, MSN, Yahoo, and Buzzfeed. Her best-selling holiday cookie box keeps her busy as she bakes over ten thousand cookies during the holiday season.

Born and raised in Hong Kong, Fanny now lives in Vancouver, BC, with her husband, Matthew, and two children, Ethan and Maya. Fanny likes to chat with her children while baking. When she's not baking, she enjoys watching movies, reading, hosting backyard parties, and hiking.

Blog: http://ohsweetday.com/
Instagram: https://www.instagram.com/oh_sweet_day/
Facebook: https://www.facebook.com/ohsweetday
Twitter: https://twitter.com/oh_sweet_day
Pinterest: https://www.pinterest.com/ohsweetday/